CONTEN

Introduction — 1

Chapter 1 - The Uncle in the Attic — 5

Chapter 2 - The Red Sandstone Asylum — 23

Chapter 3 - The Mind's Eye — 33

Chapter 4 - What's In A Name?: Louis — 47

Chapter 5 - The Path To Cap Martin — 73

Chapter 6 - The Student Soldier — 99

Chapter 7 - Another Lost Boy? — 127

Chapter 8 - Inheritance — 166

Conclusion — 176

Glossary — 181

Acknowledgements — 184

Reviews — 193

Author Page — 195

DEDICATION

For Gary, Neil, Ewan, Rory, Luke, Aron, Luca, and Daisy
that they never be required to fight.

INTRODUCTION

...all that is not said, is transmitted.
Naasson Munyandamutsa[1]

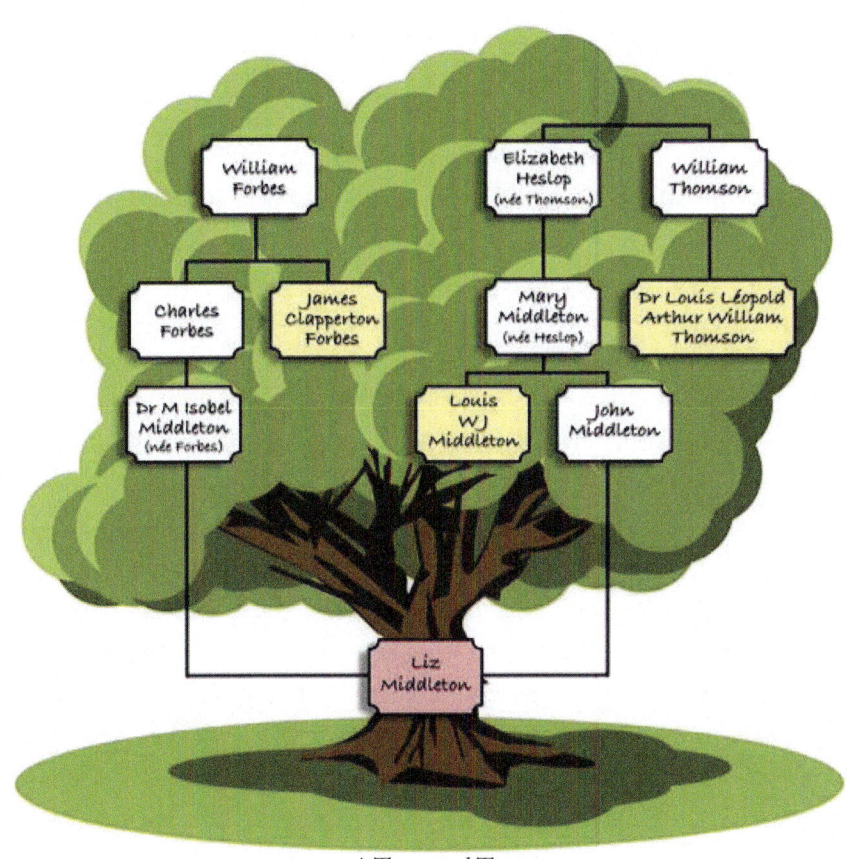

A Truncated Tree

When I was sixteen, a letter arrived at our Broughty Ferry home addressed to Louis Middleton.

'Who is Louis Middleton?' I enquired. 'Your uncle, Elizabeth'. 'What uncle?' I continued. 'Daddy's brother' replied my mother. 'What brother?' I persisted. Little of substance was revealed and so my life-long mission to find out more about this mysterious Uncle Louis began.

Stumbling upon another postal communiqué from the century before spun an ever-expanding web of intrigue. This encompassed another family man who served in the First World War, cousin Louis Thomson, seeking information about the whereabouts of Uncle Louis Middleton in France.

And rare references to James Forbes by my mother pointed to a deep well of sorrow about her uncle's loss in Belgium.

The scene was set for ensuing research that took me to different corners of the UK and Europe. The boundaries of my professional life as an orthoptist as well extended to include psychosomatic eye disorders, perhaps because I was unconsciously motivated by having a severely shell shocked uncle?

According to family lore the emigré, the enigmatic Dr Louis Léopold Arthur William Thomson had been the inconvenient child of a royal who had been adopted by the family. Coming from Upper Deeside, many of my ancestors worked in royal service, a major local employer Balmoral Castle. In a rare discussion with my mother about Louis Middleton, just after my father died, she also recalled her late uncle, James Clapperton Forbes, the second young man in this tale. Like Uncle Louis Middleton, my Great Uncle James had become a Gordon Highlander. Private James Clapperton Forbes tragically died at Ypres. My personal family history alerted me to the archaic diagnostic vestiges of the Great War in medicine, the pejorative 'malingering' judgement bestowed upon sufferers of psychosomatic eye disorders in the place of accurate diagnosis. This opened up a rewarding and ground-breaking field of enquiry and research into the 'Mind's Eye'.

The three 'brave hearts' were 2nd Lieutenant Louis William James Middleton (1896–1972) 5th Gordon Highlanders, Private James Clapperton Forbes (1894-1915) 4th Gordon Highlanders, and Dr Louis Léopold Arthur William Thomson (1879–1969), *Médecin-major*, 27th Infantry Regiment, the French Army. In not a little spirit of adventure and with a great generosity of spirit these valiant young men volunteered to contribute to their countries' war efforts. They were oblivious, I would imagine, to the hell that would behold them. As the aunt of four nephews, two great nephews and now with a little grandson, it pains me to think of the fate that can befall open-hearted young men, thinking they are doing the right thing, and nurtured as most boys are, to a greater or lesser degree, into the warrior ethos. Concluding this book during the time of the war in Ukraine in 2022 has further focused my mind.

In this often painful story these scientifically-educated young men had some shared experiences; their histories sometimes weaving in and out of each other's lives; in other ways their trajectories could not have been more different. Scotland is a small country, and by virtue of their origins in the same North Eastern corner of Scotland – Aberdeenshire and Banffshire – they had varying points of contact through kinship, educational institution, profession and regiment. For example, Uncle Louis Middleton and Uncle James Forbes, both full of promise, were students at Aberdeen University, and both joined the local regiment, the Gordon Highlanders – the 'finest regiment in the world' according to Winston Churchill.[2] And the two cousins called Louis, Uncle Louis Middleton and cousin Louis Thomson were both medical men, although the war scuppered medical student Louis Middleton's future academic and practising prospects. James Forbes and Louis Middleton were later connected by marriage, when my mother, Mary Isobel Forbes, married my father, John Middleton, during the Second World War.

I was never to meet these three family men. Had I done so, I would have, in the family tradition, called them all 'Uncle'. By the end of the First World War the outcomes of these three promising, good looking, young family men were very different. For the two Gordon Highlanders, Louis Middleton and James Forbes, their short wars ended in tragedy: Louis Middleton was so severely shell shocked at the Somme that he never recovered. James Forbes fell at Ypres, probably gassed. In the case of the third, Franco-Scot Louis Thomson, the outcome was something completely different. He survived harrowing Balkan ordeals - the typhus pandemic in Serbia and the Serbian Great

Retreat over the mountains to the Adriatic Sea - and went on to continuing professional and personal fulfilment in France. Dr Louis Thomson left behind a tale of intrigue that would not be out-of-place from the pen of John Buchan or Ian Fleming, or even from his namesake, Robert Louis Stevenson. By virtue of his survival and longevity, the tale I offer about Louis Thomson is longer than that which could be afforded by the other two's tragically truncated lives.

With time however, and many journeys, physical and emotional, shapes of these uncles began to emerge from the silence. My account is by nature episodic as I was negotiating work and a difficult life at the same time. And because of the pain and secrecy surrounding these family issues, and the variety and complexity of these men's lives, my account is not necessarily sequential in its progress nor proportionately representative. Nor do I claim this is necessarily an exhaustive family history nor any other history for that matter. It is more an impressionistic account of how ghosts from the past have haunted me – and ultimately inspired a search for something more substantive. Wherever possible I have supported my discoveries with evidence and illustrations.

I do not intend that the 'Truncated Tree' be considered a Family Tree. Descending as I do from large Victorian families, a family tree would have been a major project in itself. (It may be something I might undertake in the future.) The Truncated Tree is purely to show the relationship of these three remarkable men to each other – and to me. I hope no family members are offended by not being included.

REFERENCES

[1]*Munyandamutsa, N Cited in Wolynn, M (2016) It didn't start with you. New York: Penguin.*
[2]*http://www.gordonhighlanders.com/The-Finest-Regiment-in-the-World#.WldueMtI.GP8. Searched 11 January 2018.*

CHAPTER 1

THE UNCLE IN THE ATTIC

Am I no' a bonny fechter? Robert Louis Stevenson[1]

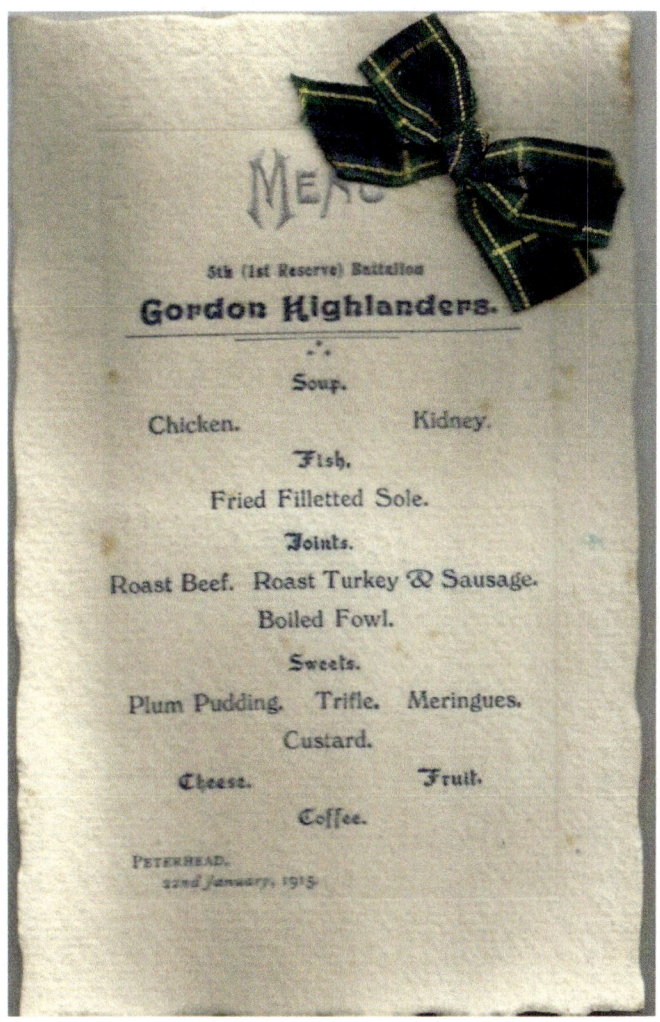

Fund-raising dinner in Peterhead for the 5th Gordon Highlanders

When I was sixteen, a letter arrived at our Broughty Ferry home addressed to Louis Middleton.

'Who is Louis Middleton?' I enquired.

'Your uncle, Elizabeth.'

'What uncle?' I continued.

'Daddy's brother,' replied my mother.

'What brother?' I persisted.

And so, in 1964, a tantalising and yet terrifying scenario was set for life. Trapped in a familial taboo on discussing painful subjects, I retreated into my father's forbidding yet fragile silence and my mother's protective stoicism. Why was this uncle missing? Was this missing relative mad? Was his madness hereditary? Why had I never heard of him? Desperate for information, at the same time I was terrified of the truth. Poking about in a cupboard I found a Gordon Highlander's bonnet and a medal. What was it all about?

THE SOUND OF SILENCE

Silence like a cancer grows Paul Simon[2]

Caught up amongst my parents' inchoate grief (there were other family war tragedies) my tense bewilderment grew. I suffered an angst-ridden adolescence, wondering if the guys in white coats would come to take me away too. I packed a wee green suitcase before going to see the family doctor.

'It's anxiety Elizabeth; take some of these.'

Phew! And yet…I was still troubled.

And so it was not until after the death of my father in 1986 that I could engage my mother further about her missing brother-in-law. By then I had established from a more forthcoming source that Uncle Louis had fought in the First World War and had been buried in a trench for days when six of his pals had been killed. He had suffered severe shell shock and spent the rest of his life in a psychiatric institution, the Crichton Royal Hospital in Dumfries. My informant was my father's and uncle's feisty sibling, retired nursing sister Maisie McKichan, who had run away from home to be a nurse, and who lived to be a hundred. Auntie Maisie's beloved battle-scarred brother Louis had been her hero.

FLOWERS OF THE FOREST

Dear, brave boys Tom Pow[3]

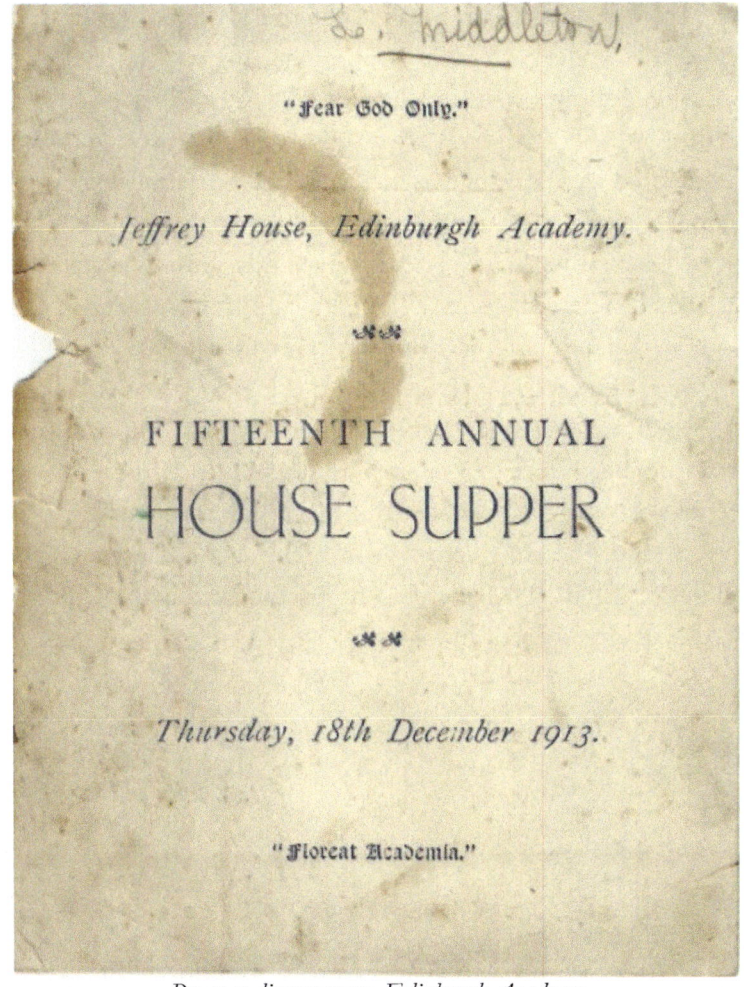

Pre-war dinner menu, Edinburgh Academy

Young Louis was educated at Edinburgh Academy, as was Secretary of State for War, Richard Haldane. Incidentally – or perhaps influentially – so was Robert Louis Stevenson. Haldane, the father of the Territorial Army, set up the Officer Training Corps in 1907. When the winds of war were blowing he returned to his *alma mater* and in a rousing speech said he looked to 'the young brains of the nation' for a reserve of officers. He invited the pupils 'to take a serious view of the duty that might someday be incumbent on them, to fight and if necessary die for the Empire.' [4]

In 1914, like his father (my grandfather) Louis began studying medicine in Aberdeen. A quiet young man, his recreational pursuits were fishing, golf and stamp collecting, but Alan Breck's refrain 'Am I no a bonny fechter?' from R L Stevenson's Kidnapped (a novel that was as revered as the Bible by the men in the family) would have reverberated through young Louis' mind, as it had his younger brother's – my father's. I too, often heard this refrain quoted. By the end of 1915 Louis was commissioned as a 2nd lieutenant in the 5th Gordon Highlanders, the Buchan Territorials, in which my grandfather also served.

The 5th Gordons trained for war in Bedford. On 4 July 1916 Uncle Louis wrote his last letter to my grandparents before sailing for France. He was staying at the Strand Place Hotel opposite the Savoy on the Strand, where three years previously fellow Edinburgh Academical, Richard Haldane, had urged the scientists of the day to work towards the unity of humanity.

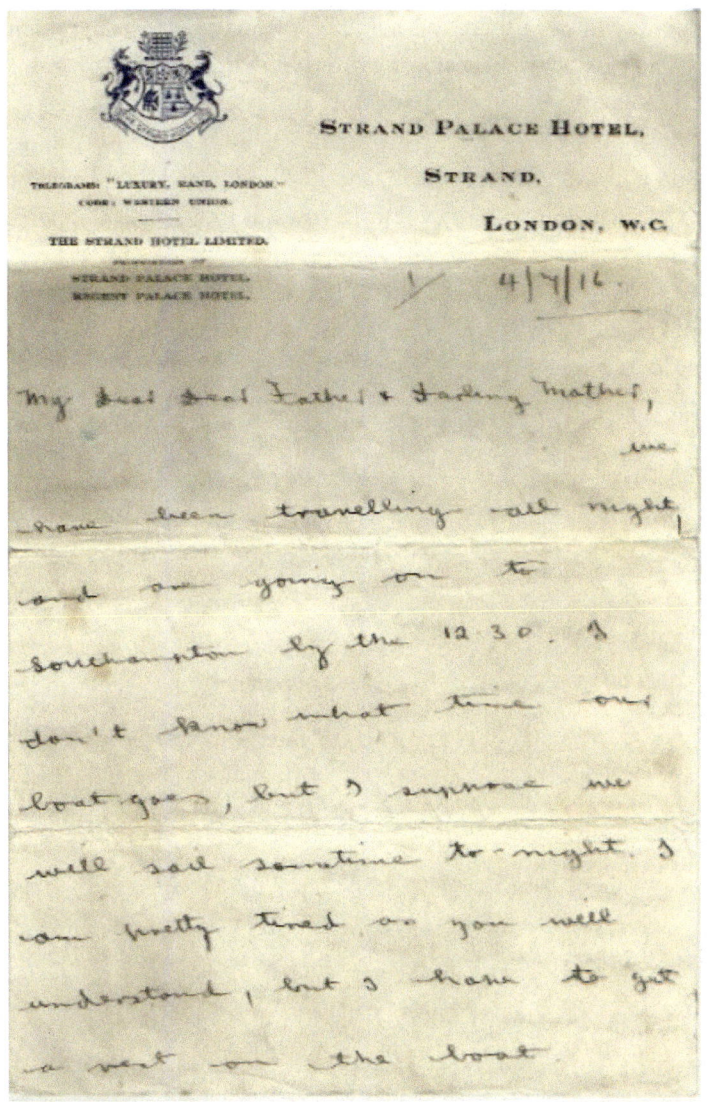

The last letter Uncle Louis wrote to his parents, before leaving for France

His letter continues:

> I saw Uncle Willie and Auntie Adelaide at Montrose, and received cigarettes from them. I saw Uncle Alex and his wife at Edinburgh, and received cigarettes, sweets etc from them. We did not pass Burton, so I did not see Uncle Charlie.

By the way Mother there was something you told me to remember, but I can't remember the exact words: you said a botany prof. said it to his class. I would like to remember the exact words.

I have something to say to you Father. I met Dr Hynd in Aberdeen Station and had a talk with him, and he said it was far too much for you to do all your work by yourself, so I think you should take it as easy as possible…

I will be looking forward to lots of letters as they fairly cheer me up. Hoping everybody is well and give my love to everybody.'

Your loving son,
Louis

Uncle Louis' last pre-war round of golf

Five days later, on 9 July 1916 – the day of my father's thirteenth birthday – 2nd Lieutenant Louis William James Middleton, 5th Gordon Highlanders, left for France. The east coast Scot played a last round of golf the day before his departure, sailing from Folkestone to Boulogne on the SS Invicta.

SS Invicta, the ship that transported the 5th Gordon Highlander to France

FRANCE

They were too keen of course, boys blown to pieces. John Glenday[5]

In no time at all the young subaltern was in the thick of war, serving at Delville Wood, Longueval and High Wood from July to November 1916. These were small pieces of bitterly fought-over land, strewn with the graves of so many young braves. High Wood is now gentle and slightly undulating land, with houses dotted about here and there, rather redolent of West Sussex. According to the Gordon Highlanders' Museum, the Gordons were also in reserve in Happy Valley, which was heavily shelled.[6] My cousin in Canada, Alasdair McKichan, who is older than me, knew Uncle Louis, and recalled in a letter how the young subaltern suffered the great terror of trench warfare, that of being entombed and buried alive.[7]

I scoured my late father's papers for further information, hoping to find Louis' letters and diaries from the trenches. Nothing. I implored other cousins to search their attics. Nothing – until 30 March 2017, when searching through some family documents for one thing (not found) I discovered another. Nearly a century later, a posting from the trenches, dated 20 July 1916:

> …*We dug shallow trenches in the wood and lived in them for seven days. I had two very narrow squeaks as the wood was regularly searched for batteries by the Huns. A shell burst about thirty feet away from me and blew me clean head over heels into my trench. What a shaking I got. I picked myself up very gently and wondered if I had been hit but I was absolutely untouched. Two of my men behind me were killed and two wounded – but not badly. How I escaped being hit beats me and after thirty minutes I was quite over the concussion.*
> *The other occasion was when a whizz bang dropped about ten feet away fortunately on marshy ground which smothered it. I had just time to throw myself on my face and I got plastered with mud but nothing more. This shell is a very small one and doesn't do much damage except at a close range. There is too much explosive in it. Although we got regularly peppered we had no more casualties.*

But our own bombardment was terrific. For nine days on end, shells of all sizes were being dropped on the Boshe (sic) lines. The roar of the guns and screeching of shells was awful but not so terrible as depicted in the papers. It has the curious effect of making me intensely sleepy. I could sleep at any time and anywhere. The last three hours before the attack was absolute Hades. The Bosche (sic) lines were one mass of smoke and flame and the whole place was trembling like an earthquake. Three days before the attack I was able to move into our medical dug out. We had accommodation for seventy-two stretcher cases and had to evacuate them for half a mile… where cars picked them up. These dug outs were decidedly shaky and at the beginning of the attack a mine explosion made it rock and I expected we were to be buried…
With my first squad I was completely buried by a shell explosion and was dug out by some Bedfords. Luckily for me my head and shoulders were clear and but for bruises was all right, but two of the men had to be sent down with shell shock or fear – they could hardly stand for shaking. The other two lost their heads and disappeared into the brushwood and have never been seen since. I searched for them but the next shell must have taken them off with a direct hit.

The 5th Gordons' pattern of trench warfare had been established. It is unclear when the damage to Louis' psyche set in. In her book, *Shell Shocked Britain*, Suzie Grogan suggests that the men who volunteered were breaking down within a month of war.[8]

Later, these Buchan boys, as part of the celebrated 51st Highland Division, went into trenches at Beaumont Hammel, at the Battle of the Ancre. Field Marshal Douglas Haig wanted to launch one last push on 24 October. Rain, mist and saturated ground delayed proceedings. The attack finally began on 13 November 1916.[9]

The Gordons' battle song, sung to the tune of 'John Brown's Body' was:

Broch birks, Ellon Stirks, Deveron to the sea,
Fite coo, Moggans blue, the rale Aldmeldrum tee,
Maud Stots, Mormond Shots…
We're the Buchan humlie breed.

Dinna think we're safties kis we get the name o' Jocks,
Dinna think we're quinies tho' ye see oor legs in frocks,

Dinna think we're frichtened at the Hun and his coal box,
We're the Buchan Humlie breed.

It is not known if they were still in good voice by the end of 1916, but it is worth recalling that one Lance Corporal Adolf Hitler, who fought at Ypres during the First World War, had referred to the Highland regiments as the 'Ladies from hell'.

Memorial to the 51st Highland Division, towering over Y Ravine, France

The Gordon Highlanders' war diary for 22 October 1916 details how 2nd Lieutenant Middleton led a party of soldiers placing

Bangalore torpedoes in the German wire so that a raiding party could penetrate the German strongpoint.[10]

Trenches near Y Ravine, Beaumont Hamel, France, 2014

Delayed by the terrible weather and the attendant 'sod'[11] the brigade eventually launched its attack on 13 November – their objective being Y Ravine. They were under the command of Major-General George 'Uncle' Harper. The successful completion of this assault was strategically important and a prerequisite for the morale of the 51st Highland Division. The 29th Division had lost 5115 casualties when attacking the same position on 1 July. The 51st Highland Division, by contrast, lost less than half that number: there were 2200 casualties killed, wounded or missing at Y Ravine. Furthermore, their previous failure to take High Wood had earned them the unwelcome nickname 'Harper's Duds'. Harper, however, was heard to overhear one of the walking wounded making his way back to the line after this battle saying 'Onyway, they winna ca' us Hairper's Duds noo'.

Their objective was taken, and by 19 November 1916 (which would have been my mother's third birthday) the bloodiest battle in British military history, the Battle of the Somme, was over. The 51st Highland Division was acknowledged by the Germans as 'one of the crack infantry formations in the British Army'.[12] According to Major F W Bewsher, author of *The History of the 51st Highland Division*,[13] the Battle of Beaumont-Hamel was the foundation stone on which the reputation of the 51st Highland Division was built. Although I am essentially an opponent of war, believing it to be a breakdown in humanity, I cannot help but feel proud of the massive contribution of my brave Uncle Louis and his fellow Gordons and the 51st Highland Division.

The author in front of Y Ravine, Beaumont Hamel, France

THE PITY OF WAR

But broken, broken, broken
Are the sons of the heather
E A Mackintosh [14]

Louis was severely shell shocked and 'evacuated sick'. All mention of him in the Gordon Highlanders' war diary ends at the conclusion of the Battle of the Somme, November 1916. Thereafter his history becomes hazy. Where had he been from 1916 to 1919, between the Somme and his admission to the Crichton?

My search for Louis was long and convoluted. It took me to different corners of Scotland, England, France and Belgium. One of my first ports of call was the site of the old Craiglockhart War Hospital on the outskirts of Edinburgh, but I could find no trace of my uncle there. I don't think that he ever had been, but I was nevertheless fortunate in being able to visit the old hydropathic hotel that had housed the hospital before its conversion to modern university use. In the 1990s it was much as it would have been at the time of its celebrated poet-patients, Wilfred Owen, Siegfried Sassoon and Robert Graves. With its long dark corridors, it had a quiet, glaucous aspect to it. Sassoon had poetically described it as 'a gloomy cavernous place'[15]. The kind archivist allowed me to look at original documents by the poets, including the magazine, *Hydra,* which was once edited by Owen, and included poems by Sassoon. I returned to Craiglockhart in 2017 for a conference to commemorate the centenary of the meeting there of Owen and Sassoon. It had been transformed into a modern academic institution.

Craiglockhart War Hospital offered a glimmer of light amongst much darkness. Here innovatory war doctor, W H R Rivers, offered solace and understanding to shell shocked officers. Siegfried Sassoon had a high regard for Rivers: 'There was never any doubt about my liking him. He made me feel safe at once and seemed to know all about me.'[16] In his poem *Revisitation 1934, Dr W H R Rivers*[17] Sassoon reflected:

> *What voice revisits me this night? What face*
> *To my heart's room returns?*
> *From the perpetual silence where the grace*
> *Of human sainthood burns*
> *Hastes he once more to harmonise and heal?*

I know not. Only I feel
His influence undiminished
And his life's work, in me and man, unfinished.

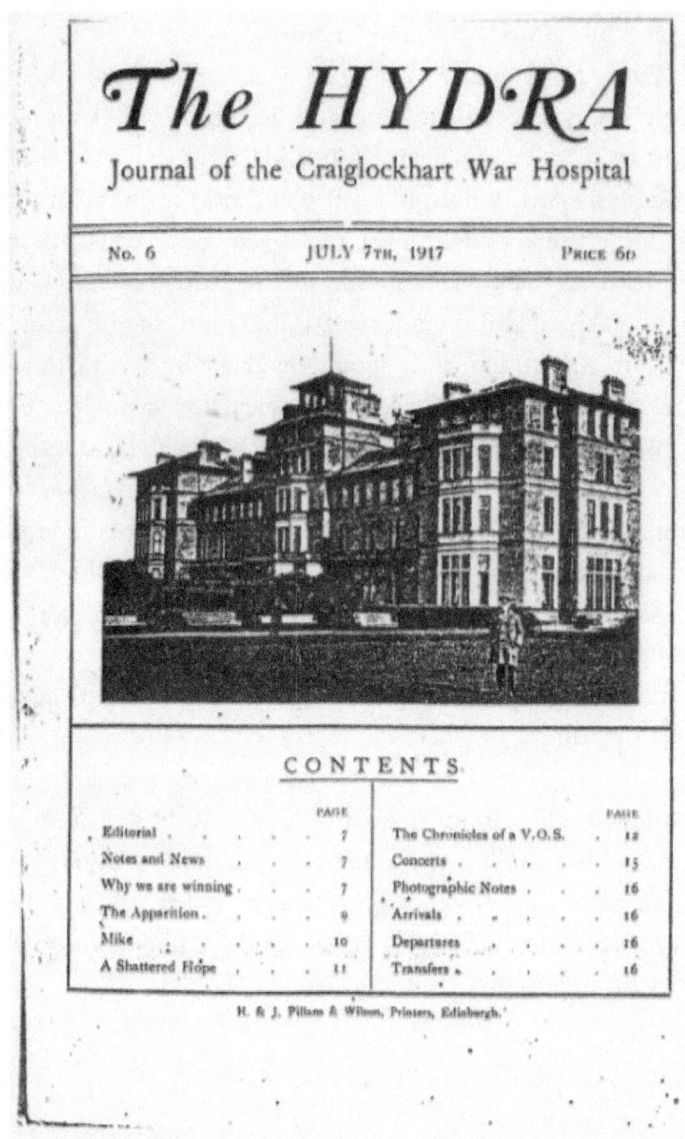

Magazine produced by in-patients at Craiglockhart War Hospital

But to return to my search for Uncle Louis, I found in my father's papers a letter dated 23 February 1919 from an officer in the 5th Gordons in Germany to my grandfather, who was searching at the time for information about his son. This, too, yielded little information. Reading between the lines, however, it appears to me that my grandfather had wanted to know if Louis had resigned his commission – or had been required to. The underlying male Middleton issue it would seem was whether or not the first-born son was indeed 'a bonny fechter'.

Uncle Louis' medical discharge employment card

What is clear is that the battle-scarred war hero never recovered, and for over half a century whiled away his hours in a psychiatric hospital. I have striven over the years to fill in the gaps in my uncle's heroic (in the terms of the day) and ultimately sacrificial tale. I learned that Louis had had two periods of hospitalisation before coming back permanently to Scotland in late 1919 - and that sometime after the Somme he had joined the motor transport section of the Royal Flying Corps and had been in the Army Reserve B.

5th Gordon Highrs
Strempt.
Germany
23.2.19.

Dear Doctor,

Since my return we have been on the move practically every day and have arrived at the above named place. This morning I went into the office and saw the record of service book, and can find only the following particulars.

Date of joining, temporarily attached to Trench Mortar Battery and, evacuated sick. The number of some Army Order is also stated and I have written the base to find out what it refers to. So far as I can find out, had there been any particular cause for L— being compelled to resign his commission, this would have been entered.

As soon as I get Col. McDonald's confidential reply I'll forward it along with any other papers.

The following is the address of the M.O. who was with the battalion at the

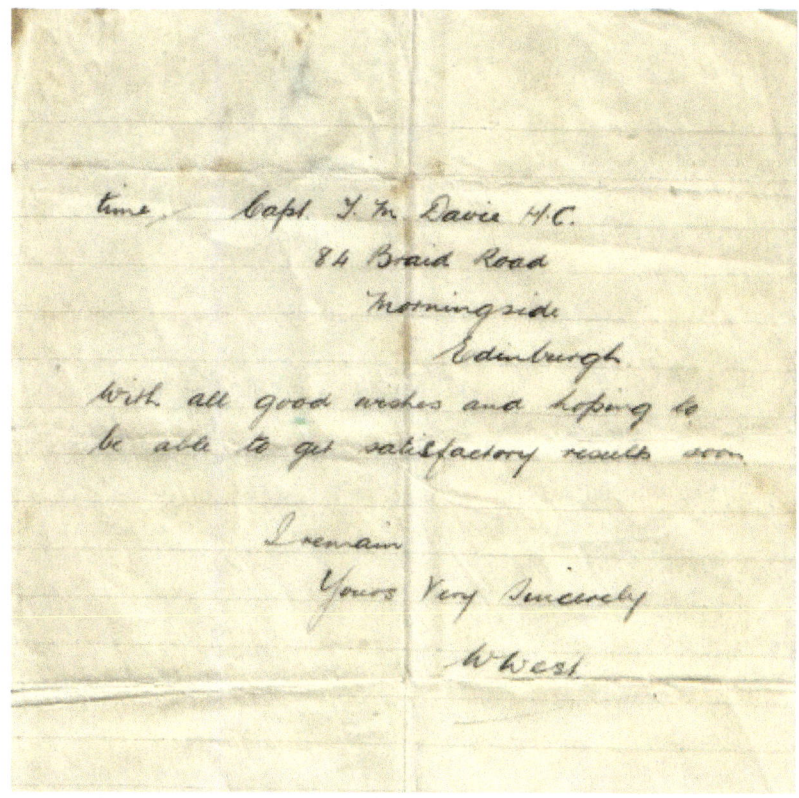

Letter to my grandfather from W West, an officer in the 5th Gordons, Strempt, Germany, 23 February 1919

The exact chronology of these periods is lost in the fog of war and varies in different records. He was finally discharged from the army on 22 February 1918 as 'being no longer physically fit for war service'. The psychologically damaged soldiers were often described as being physically unfit rather than mentally unwell, which contributed to the statistical under-representation of shell shock, although on another document Louis was unequivocally described as 'insane'.

REFERENCES

[1] Stevenson, R L (1886) *Kidnapped.* London: Cassell and Company Limited.

[2] Simon, P *The sound of silence.*

[3] Pow, T (2008) *'Service Patient, 1916. Dear Alice: Narratives of madness'.* Cambridge: Salt Publishing.

[4] Strachan, H (2014) *Haldane, Haig and Hamilton: The mobilisation of Scotland in 1914.* The Caledonian Club.

[5] Glenday, J *The lost boy. Modern poets on Viking poetry: an anthology of responses to Skaldic Poetry* ed. Debbie Potts 2013. Filmpoem: Sonatorrek (Loss of Sons)

[6] Ross, MI (1 September 2014) Private communication. Gordon Highlanders Museum.

[7] McKichan, A (8 September 2014) Letter.

[8] Grogan, S (2014) *Shell shocked Britain.* Barnsley: Pen & Sword History.

[9] Royle, T (2006) *The flowers of the forest.* Edinburgh: Birlinn Ltd.

[10] Ross, M1 (1 September 2014) Private communication. Gordon Highlanders Museum.

[11] Symon, M (1938) *A recruit for the Gordons* IN *Deveron days.* Aberdeen: D Wyllie & Son.

[12] Royle, T (2006)

[13] Bewsher, FW, (1921) *The history of the 51st (Highland) Division* Edinburgh and London: William Blackwood and Sons

[14] Mackintosh, EA (1918) *To the 51st Division: High Wood, July-August 1916* IN *War, the liberator and other pieces.* London: John Lane, the Bodley Head, 1918.

[15] Sassoon, S (1941) *The complete memoirs of George Sherston.* London Faber and Faber.

[16] Sassoon, S (1941)

[17] Sassoon, S (1935) *Revisitation 1934, Dr W H Rivers. In Vigilis.* London: William Heinemann Ltd.

CHAPTER 2

THE RED SANDSTONE ASYLUM

In these, the great asylums of Scotland, always it is evening about to fall. The heavy doors are closing on us all Tom Pow[1]

Easterbrook Hall, the Crichton Royal Hospital

My Uncle Louis spent over fifty years – from 1919 until his death in 1972 – in the Crichton Royal Psychiatric Hospital in Dumfries. Just after the death of my father, a uniquely poignant time in 1986, I asked my mother, 'Did Dad ever visit Uncle Louis?' 'No,' said my mother, 'it upset him too much.' I never did establish who was too upset, my father or my uncle. On raising the subject with my brother in 2015, he didn't know either.

The church, the Crichton © Andrew C J Middleton 2016

The word 'Crichton' entered my lexicon of Gothic horror. Mention of the now innocuous-sounding Glasgow University Crichton Campus still has the power to chill. The red sandstone Victorian institution, high on the outskirts of town, now also houses that most banal of twenty-first-century workplaces, the call centre. Coincidentally, Louis' great-nephew, my nephew, Neil Middleton, worked there in student vacations from 2004-06.

> 'Let us remember' he begins, 'what's most remarkable about the very room we're in tonight - only last year it was home to the criminally insane.' [2]

Galloway House, one of Louis' wards, more recently the call centre for a company providing bedside hospital media services

I sometimes wonder if those university graduates and undergraduates who work at this call centre ever consider the practices that once took place on the site. The Crichton Royal Hospital, founded in 1833 from a bequest left by a local widow, Elizabeth Crichton,[3] was one of the more comfortable asylums of its time. Under the stewardship of Dr W A F Browne, it adopted a more progressive approach to the care of the mentally ill, incorporating activities that might be considered the forerunners of occupational therapy, such as amateur dramatics and a hospital newsletter. In the middle of the twentieth century, it was considered by some, but not the author, to be psychiatrically innovative incorporating methods such as electroconvulsive therapy and prefrontal leucotomies.[4] I have not been able to find evidence that psychotherapy or psychoanalysis were on offer; certainly I discovered Louis received neither, but Charcot, the French neurologist and pioneer in the use of hypnosis with hysteria, apparently visited the Crichton in 1879,[5] as did Freud in 1939. Freud declared:

Lord there's a whole nation waiting for the couch. [6]

I finally crossed the Rubicon in the early nineties and rang the Crichton Royal Hospital. My trembling hand clutching the receiver, I asked 'Could you provide information about my late uncle, your patient, Louis W J Middleton who died in your care in 1972?' 'No,' I was told. 'There is a fifty-year rule.'

Fifty years! I could be dead! My disappointment was palpable. Alternately tantalised and terrified by a vague awareness of a mad uncle, I had been garnering courage to make this call for decades. Having discovered I had an uncle locked away in this remote asylum I had to find out more information about him for my own peace of mind. My quest faltered, however, thwarted at the first hurdle.

Of course, medical professionals have to consider patient confidentiality. I am a health professional myself and I understand this. However, I was the next of kin and the patient was dead. My younger brother, my only sibling, who coincidentally lived in Dumfries, demonstrated no interest in the subject. I was no threat as far as I could see. *Au contraire*, I was a professional with a research interest in psychosomatic eye disorders. To no avail – my plight cut little ice with the old guard at the Crichton Royal.

SHELL SHOCK

These are men whose minds the Dead have ravished. [7]

With the Crichton doors firmly shut, I sought to expand my understanding of shell shock and the First World War. A burst of fictional accounts of the war emerged as that most destructive of centuries, the twentieth, approached its end. I was especially absorbed by the works of Pat Barker[8] and Sebastian Faulks[9] – and there were always, of course, the remarkable war poets.

> *No doubt they'll soon get well; the shock and strain*
> *Have caused their stammering, disconnected talk.*

> *Of course they're 'longing to go out again,'* –
> *These boys with old, scared faces, learning to walk.*
> *They'll soon forget their haunted nights: their cowed*
> *Subjection to the ghosts of friends who died,* –
> *Their dreams that drip with murder; and they'll be proud*
> *Of glorious war that shatter'd all their pride ...*
> *Men who went out to battle, grim and glad;*
> *Children, with eyes that hate you, broken and mad.* [10]

Siegfried Sassoon's optimistic poem, set in Craiglockhart Hospital for Officers in Edinburgh, assumed recovery from shell shock. The decorated 2nd Lieutenant Sassoon, however, was not truly affected by battle neurosis; nor was he at the time a pacifist. Instead, he didn't like how the war was being run and had thrown his Military Cross into the River Mersey.[11] Sassoon had been sent to 'Dottyville' in 1917, as he referred to Craiglockhart, to have his attitude 'adjusted'.[12] Also there at that time was fellow poet Wilfred Owen, who had actually broken down.

Pat Barker's *Regeneration* novels also describe Craiglockhart and the more enlightened pioneering treatment of psychologically war-damaged men which was carried out there by W H R Rivers, as well as the more troubling approaches employed elsewhere. I took myself off in 1993 to the Napier University Library in Edinburgh (on the site of the former hospital) to see if Uncle Louis had been a patient at Craiglockhart. He hadn't. The reality for most shell shocked men was not necessarily where the 'kind lamp shone', as Robert Graves described the presence of early psychoanalyst, Rivers.[13] (Graves had accompanied Sassoon to Craiglockhart, and remained a friend of Rivers all his life.) Instead, in many other hospitals, shell shocked men were at the mercy of another kind of war doctor.

FROM WHITE COATS TO WHITE DRESSES

At my request, interested consultant psychiatric colleagues wrote to the Crichton supporting my appeal for information about Uncle

Louis. Doctors like speaking to doctors. The Crichton however, didn't agree with the usefulness of my knowing about my uncle, neither personally nor professionally. Later, however, when I was participating in multi-disciplinary research into Psychosomatic Eye Disorders, another colleague wrote to the Crichton supporting my application to find out about Uncle Louis. A little glimmer of light came shining back from the land of locked wards! I was to be granted a guarded audience with a consultant at the Crichton. And so in 1994, my bright nine-year-old Dumfries-born nephew Gary, directed me to the Crichton (where he would later embark on his psychiatric placement as a medical student).

Gary waited in the car with my husband as I made my wary way up the grand staircase in the Crichton's Queensberry West, my knees threatening to buckle under me. In front of the consultant psychiatrist were my shell shocked uncle's case notes. On the desk, most movingly and tantalisingly, was also a letter from Louis' father, my grandfather, Dr James Middleton, to Dr Easterbrook. I never knew my paternal grandfather.

My grandfather died in 1920, aged only sixty-eight, a year after Louis had been committed to the Crichton. This was many years before I was born. I had never before or since seen a letter from my famously eloquent grandfather, student of Robert Louis Stevenson, but a copy of his letter was not to be forthcoming.

Dr James Middleton, Uncle Louis' father and my grandfather

The psychiatrist read that old Dr Middleton was a well-respected family doctor and he did not want his 'insane' son nearby in Aberdeenshire. As I feared, shame and stigma had reared their ugly heads and caused the life-long rejection of the damaged war hero; he had sacrificed his mental health for his country, and had been banished to a faraway psychiatric institution. Dumfries could not be further in Scotland from Peterhead, especially in the early twentieth century. To this day, Dumfries remains off the beaten track and is still hard to reach. I can attest to this after years of visiting my brother and nephews there and laterally my elderly mother who moved there from the east coast.

Since my first visit to the Crichton the estate's use has extended to include university buildings, a hotel and an events' venue. The eponymous Easterbrook Hall, one-time home of the surgical theatre where prefrontal leucotomies would have been carried out, is now marketed as 'Your Dream Wedding Destination'.[14]

Easterbrook Hall, now a wedding and events venue

On the site of the hitherto hydrotherapy pool there is now a spa, which is open to the public. This adjoins the convivial 'Neuro's Café', which I first encountered in 2016 when attending some dear friends' nearby wedding. Whilst in Dumfries for another wedding in 2021 (for that of my third nephew, Ewan to Rebecca) the spa and café complex had been renamed the 'Easterbrook Bistro, Bar and Spa'.

Neuro's Café, now the Easterbrook Bar and Bistro

I had arranged to stay at the Holiday Inn on the Crichton estate during the 2021 wedding visit. This I discovered was not a good idea. This is no reflection on the hotel which was perfectly comfortable, but staying in the former psychiatric hospital grounds was an unsettling emotional demand too far for this niece of a former long-term in-patient. More psychologically manageable were the more traditional venues where we stayed at the weddings of my other nephews, Gary, Neil and Rory.

Remaining Crichton Royal hospital original features: tiles of the time, now part of the Dumfries Holiday Inn

REFERENCES

[1] Pow T (2008) 'The Great Asylums of Scotland' in *Dear Alice. Narratives of Madness.* Cambridge: Salt Publishing.

[2] Pow (2008) 'Inauguration'.

[3] Wellcome Library (2016) 'Crichton Royal Hospital'. Available at: http://wellcomelibrary.org/collections/digital-collections/mental-healthcare/crichton-royal-hospital/ (Accessed 30 April 2016).

[4] Smith, M (February 2010) 'State of Mind', *Dumfries & Galloway Life.*

[5] Pow (2008) 'Charcot, Master of Salpêtrière, delivers his "Tuesday lecture"'.

[6] Pow (2008) 'Freud at the Crichton. Home movie September 1939'.

[7] Owen, W (1918) 'Mental cases' in Motion, A (2003) *First World War Poems.* London: Faber & Faber Ltd.

[8] Barker, P (1991) *Regeneration.* London: Viking.

[9] Faulks, S (1993) *Birdsong.* London: Hutchinson.

[10] Sassoon S (1919) 'Survivors' in *The war poems of Siegfried Sassoon.* London: Heinemann.

[11] Murray, N (2012) *The Red Sweet Wine of Youth: the Brave and Brief Lives of the War Poets.* London: Little Brown.

[12] Graves, R (1923) 'The Red Ribbon Dream' in *Whipperginny.* London: Heinemann, in Slobodin, R (1978) *WHR Rivers: Pioneer Anthropologist, Psychiatrist of the Ghost Road.* New York City: Columbia University Press.

[13] Slobodin (1978)

[14] Easterbrook Hall: Your Dream Wedding Destination. Available at: http://www.easterbrookhall.co.uk/weddings/ (Accessed 30 April 2016).

CHAPTER 3

THE MIND'S EYE

*Therefore still their eyeballs shrink formulated
Back into their brains* Wilfred Owen[1]

Note viewing windows on doors of what were patients' rooms, in one of Uncle Louis Middleton's former wards, Grierson House (now commercial offices)

If shell shock is the prism through which much of the cultural history of the 1914–18 war has been viewed,[2] then the 'malingering' diagnosis is a lens through which we may regard the progression of holistic twentieth-century medicine.

Concurrent with my search for Louis' tale, my personal concern for him and his suffering informed my professional focus as a clinical orthoptist. Orthoptics, the diagnosis and treatment of disorders of the extra-ocular muscles, is a precise scientific classification system employing largely quantitative diagnostic techniques; the methodology is less orientated towards qualitative analysis. I became curious, however, when no physical reason was found to account for patients' loss of sight, and I was not satisfied that the traditional response addressed patients' needs. To my dismay, the default ophthalmological diagnosis for patients in the eye clinic where no physical clinical sign had been found was 'malingering or hysterical'. This was a vestige of the First World War's military doctors' prejudice, rather than sound clinical assessment. Here judgement masqueraded as diagnosis.[3]

The malingering 'diagnosis' had an ignoble history. Those so labelled during the First World War could be shot at dawn or suffer barbaric field punishments. The 'treatment' at the hand of war doctors could be brutal. The more fortunate sufferers of shell shock, if they could in any way be described as fortunate, might be seen by a new breed of more sympathetic doctors like W H R Rivers and his colleague Charles Samuel Myers, a psychologist. They employed the pioneering psychoanalytic method.[4] Myers employed the term 'shell shock' in 1915 in a paper in *The Lancet*[5] although there is some debate whether or not he actually originated it. It is lamentable, however, that the archaic 'malingering' attitude endured in the eye clinic throughout the twentieth century, whereas other specialities embraced one of the century's great leaps forward, the recognition of the influence of the unconscious mind on human behaviour.[6]

Meanwhile, I felt a professional disconnect in the eye clinic. The orthoptist such as me would be required to carry out prescribed test results to present to the ophthalmologist, the eye doctor. The ophthalmologist would then communicate the clinical findings to the patient's general practitioner. I was a lone voice, and I had not a body of research work to substantiate my hunches. This seemed to me such a disservice to the patient who was discharged from the ophthalmology department with the diagnosis: 'NAD: malingering or hysterical'. NAD stands for no apparent defect. (That is no found physical ophthalmological defect.) The cause for loss of vision for reasons other than physical would therefore remain unexplored and unexplained. There was a cultural and epistemological gap in vision services. To create new diagnostic and therapeutic criteria in a medical setting, new thinking had to be developed, and it had to be substantiated with an evidence base before it could be practised professionally. To my delight serendipity came my way in the mid-nineties, when an invitation to participate in the innovatory two-year, multi-disciplinary research project into 'Psychological Aspects of Eye Disorders' dropped into my letterbox.[7] This was another unexpected communiqué that afforded a turning point in my life. There was a thread of connection to the letter addressed to Louis Middleton arriving at the family home in the sixties that should hopefully become apparent in these pages, as well as to a postcard from Dr Louis Thomson in France to my grandparents as the First World War approached its end.

These research seminars were to take place at the Tavistock Clinic in Hampstead, an institute devoted to addressing psychological suffering. Dr Hugh Crichton-Miller, son of the manse, and former Great War doctor, set up the Tavie, as it is affectionately known, to respond to the emotional fall-out from that most terrible of wars. This specific study of psychosomatic eye disorders was funded by the bequest of William Inman, a First World War ophthalmic surgeon who, unusually for an ophthalmologist, became a pioneering psychoanalyst working with what could be called 'shell blindness'. Bill Inman, as he was known, practised at the Queen Alexandra Hospital, in Portsmouth, on the south coast of England. He treated men sent over from the Western Front who couldn't see, but had no identifiable physical clinical eye disorder to account for their loss of vision.[8] This puzzled the good doctor.

The research seminars in which I participated were organised along the lines of the Balint method,[9] whereby the professionals were encouraged to think about the meaning of their patients' presenting symptoms. They arose after Dr Sotiris Zalidis, a general practitioner with an interest in psychological medicine, invited Dr Alexis Brook, a psychoanalytic psychotherapist, to the surgery where Dr Zalidis worked as a principal, to conduct the primary care part of his research into emotional aspects of eye disorders. Their ten-year collaboration included these pioneering Balint-style multidisciplinary research eye groups that they co-led with Dr Andrew Elder at the Tavistock Clinic. Dr Brook had already carried out research into the meaning of eye disorders in Inman's old department in Portsmouth.[10] Our multi-disciplinary seminar participants included ophthalmologists, orthoptists like myself, optometrists, general practitioners, a teacher for visually impaired children, psychotherapists, social workers working with visually impaired clients, and workers in voluntary organisations for those who were blind and partially sighted.

From this cradle, the role of the unconscious was explored in a safe and supportive setting, and later tentatively introduced into diagnostic and therapeutic thinking in the eye clinic. This was neither an easy task nor a popular departure amongst my professional colleagues: Indeed, it could provoke hostility, as in, for example, the response 'I am only interested in the eyes' when I suggested to a colleague the possible effect of a patient's severe distress on his presenting symptoms. I was swimming against the tide, and this in a reductive and prescriptive National Health Service clinical culture as the end of the twentieth century approached. For the troubled patient, however, the more expansive approach could be transformative. It shifted the focus of professional interest from the redundant notion of conscious 'malingering' into the governing effect of the distress-rendered unconscious, and opened up the possibility of understanding the effects of trauma or conflict on vision. When required to give evidence to the Austrian war ministry during World War One, Sigmund Freud had sought to explain the moral and ethical dilemma facing the soldier:

> *Psychoanalysis ... has taught ... that peacetime neurosis can be traced back to disturbances in a person's emotional life. The same explanation has now been generally applied to those suffering from war neuroses ... the immediate cause of all war neuroses was a soldier's unconscious inclination to remove himself from the aspects of military service that are dangerous or offensive to his feelings. Fear*

for his own life, resistance to the command to kill others, revolt against the total suppression of one's personality by superiors were the most important emotional sources that nourished the inclination to shun war. A healthy soldier in whom these emotional motives were to become powerfully and clearly conscious would either desert or report himself sick. But only a small fraction of war neurotics were actually simulators: the emotional impulse against military service that arose in them and drove them to be sick operated in them without their being conscious of it.[11] *[author's italics]*

The seminars were ground breaking. Coming from a range of professions, the participants – and consequently their patients and their clients - benefited from the different perspectives on visual and ocular disorders. When the seminars finished, I was inspired to propose and participate in organising the highly successful *Mind's Eye* series of conferences[12] with some of the other participants and then set up *The Eye and the Mind Society*.

Also, in spite of a number of cultural and institutional challenges, I eventually established, along with colleagues in psychological medicine, the first-ever Mind's Eye Clinic at University College London Hospitals. Patients seen in the eye clinic with reduced vision or diminished focusing power, with no apparent physical cause to account for this, apart from a history suggestive of emotional distress, could be referred directly, in-house, from eye professionals to professionals in psychological medicine.[13] In our particular case, with the referrals being within-trust, there was the added advantage of accruing no extra referral charge for the service. This clinical model could be replicated in trusts with both departments of psychological medicine and ophthalmology.

Towards the end of the twentieth century, some of the child and adult patients that I saw had come from troubled parts of the world and war-zones, such as the Lebanon, Rwanda and the former Yugoslavia. Unfortunately, my clinical managers didn't fully support this Mind's Eye Clinic model; it had taken an enormous amount of work to set up, and I was provided one clinic to my delight. My new clinical departure however was thwarted from the beginning! It was diverted back down the traditional referral route from ophthalmology to neuro-ophthalmology, which was not the intended idea at all. In fact it was the complete opposite. I was assigned to a consultant neuro-ophthalmologist. This was reminiscent of the historical ideological struggles between neurology and the nascent discipline of psychoanalysis of nearly a century before and effectively thwarted our hard-won initiative before it had become established. Nevertheless, our efforts had set a precedent, a template. Almost a century after the First World War work of William Inman, our new clinical model was recognised with the publication of our paper in *Eye,* the official scientific journal of the Royal College of Ophthalmologists and published by *Nature.*[14]

THE WAR DOCTORS

According to Sigmund Freud, 'Treatment given by a doctor under military command was inevitably confused by 'the insoluble conflict between the claims of humanity, which normally carry decisive weight for a physician, and the demands of a national war'. [15]

The celebrated French neurologists Jean-Martin Charcot, 'the Napoleon of Neurosis' [16] and Pierre Janet had been exploring the nature of 'hysteria' towards the end of the nineteenth century.[17] In the German-speaking countries, Sigmund Freud (a former pupil of Charcot), Carl Jung and Alfred Adler had been developing their theories about the mind and its disorders.[18] British army doctors, however, with their warring philosophies and prejudices around aetiology, diagnosis and treatment, were less understanding. One suspects that these sceptical island doctors with their 'unconscious insularity' [19] thought this new Continental thinking about the unconscious was some fancy foreign nonsense or some such thing. On pondering this notion, I happened upon this semi-fictionalised account of the response of the old guard to pioneering Dr Rivers' arrival at Craiglockart Hospital for Officers in Edinburgh:

> *[A] visiting commission of busybodies, arriving unexpectedly and armed with an absurd technical knowledge and jargon, insisted upon the immediate sack of the Commandant and his replacement by a civilian professor of psychology ... a man who not only believed in the existence of the subject which he professed, but also read books about it written by foreigners and Germans at that.* [20]

Along with Siegfried Sassoon, the broken-down officers sent to Craiglockhart were fortunate in encountering the sympathetic Dr William Rivers. This anthropologist, colour-vision physiologist and pioneering psychoanalyst listened to his traumatised charges' memories, with a view to de-toxifying the horror and promoting catharsis (and returning them to battle). This progressive approach existed in spite of ingrained attitudes:

> *A handful of highly qualified civilians in uniform were up against the usual red-tape ideas ... the military authorities regarded war hospitals for nervous disorders as experiments which needed careful watching and firm handling ... Rivers told me that the local director of medical services nourished a deep-rooted prejudice against Slateford [Sassoon's nom de guerre for Craiglockhart] and asserted that he 'never had and never would recognise the existence of such a thing as shell shock.* [21]

At this time war-traumatised servicemen were at the mercy of these doctors' warring whims about the causes of shell shock. Many notions, as former surgeon and later psychoanalyst Millais Culpin outlined, were 'no nearer to reality than ... the explosion of thunder ... the voice of an angry god.' [22] Their 'diagnoses' owed more to Victorian and Edwardian views about masculinity than scientific theory, along with unrealistic expectations of human endurance in the face of the terror of industrialised warfare. Culpin modestly and realistically acknowledged 'the existence of problems before which our education has left us powerless'. Prominent military doctor Colonel Frederick Mott at the Maudsley Hospital in London, however, did not display such modesty. He was instead the dominant voice in the biological and inherited view of mental illness in shell shocked soldiers, especially during the first two years of the war.

Frederick Mott had been of the view that shellfire brought structural changes to the central nervous system, causing blindness, paralysis and impairment of other senses.[23] With time however, and with the inescapable evidence of the sheer numbers of men returning psychologically damaged, some who had been nowhere near shells, Colonel Mott had to reconsider his views. As early as December 1914 reports had reached the War Office that 7–10 per cent of officers and 3–4 per cent of all ranks were being sent home in a state of nervous collapse.[24] This was almost certainly an underestimate. Mott started to contemplate the predisposition of the individual to nervous disorder, stating:

> *… by far the most important factor in the genesis of war psycho-neuroses is an inborn or acquired tendency to emotivity.*[25]

But Mott couldn't ever fully embrace the overwhelming contribution to breakdown caused by the sights, sounds and smells, the carnage, the sense of impotence and, ultimately, the terror in the trenches, in one of the worst bloodbaths in history.

Colonel Mott's avoidance-based approach promoted a cheery forward-thinking outlook, 'an atmosphere of cure' and avoiding bad memories.[26] This was quite unlike the approach of the progressive shell shock doctors like Rivers, Myers of the Royal Army Medical Corps (RAMC) in France, and Rows at the Red Cross Military Hospital in Maghull, Lancashire. Their method was to coax from their suffering charges their tormenting memories and persecuting nightmares in an effort to understand and relieve them. Hypnosis and psychoanalysis, Mott argued, were not 'necessary or even desirable'.[27] Major Rows at Maghull felt that Mott's physiological approach was 'getting in the way of something very important' and that Mott was 'somebody who ought to be opposed'.[28]

At its most gentle end, Colonel Mott's spectrum of treatment involved activities like gardening, warm baths and choral music. He believed, however, that 'discipline is very essential'.[29] The 'treatment' package also included deceit, where the shell shocked soldier was told he would not be sent back to the Front if he recovered. (He was.). I was shocked that this happened at all. I was further horrified to discover that my broken-down uncle had been returned to the Front after treatment in the UK. As well as deception, Mott employed the staging of fake operations, which involved anaesthetising and cutting patients who were led to believe this would 'cure' them.[30] He also used faradism, the application of increasingly strong and agonising electrical currents until the offending symptom disappeared.[31] The patient would not be allowed to leave the room until he spoke, or saw, or regained whatever the impaired faculty had been. As Freud clarified, the pain of the electricity had to be worse than active military service.[32]

Mott referred his 'most difficult' cases to the zealous Lewis Yealland at the National Hospital, in Queen's Square, London.[33] Flourishing faradism, Yealland saw it is as his mission to be 'an evangelist grappling with evil, driving the devils from his patient's body'.[34] Accounts of Yealland's treatment with faradism in locked rooms make for disturbing reading.[35] Along with his colleague Edgar Douglas Adrian, they ran a clinic at the National which in itself seemed designed to cause trauma. At its most extreme end it can only be described as torture.

> *The current can be made extremely painful if it is necessary to supply the disciplinary element which must be invoked if the patient is one of those who prefer not to recover, and it can be made strong enough to break down the unconscious barriers to sensation in the most profound functional anaesthesia.*[36]

I'M BEGINNING TO SEE THE LIGHT

A thin, dark man with the abrupt manner which distinguishes the army surgeon from the West End practitioner.[37]

One of Louis' former wards (Maxwell House), now part of Glasgow University

On my journey of discovery, I learnt there was a museum in Easterbrook Hall at the Crichton. (The museum no longer exists.) I made contact with the archivist who enabled me to see the wards where Louis had whiled away half a century: Grierson House, Maxwell House and Galloway House. It was a gruelling visit with a surreal touch. These erstwhile wards no longer accommodate patients. At the time of writing these buildings housed commercial offices for the Crichton Development Company Limited, some Glasgow University buildings, and the call centre for a company providing hospital bedside telephone and television services.

What a difference a century makes: Grierson House, another of Louis' former wards, now commercial offices

I then had a flash of inspiration in my search for Uncle Louis. I brought the archivist at Easterbrook Hall the last letter Louis wrote before he left for the Front: dated 4 July 1916, and written from the Strand Palace Hotel, London, it begins 'My dear dear Father and Darling Mother, and finishes 'Your loving son, Louis.' [38] She was visibly moved and I gave her a photocopy for the museum. In two minutes she had his case notes in front of me.

I read in the notes that Uncle Louis had been sent home from France in 1917 into the hands of Colonel Frederick Mott at the Maudsley Neurological Section, and that he had later been returned to the Front. My heart sank. I had not known that this was standard practice and that the aim of war doctors was to patch up and return injured servicemen to the Front. I had had no idea at the time who Colonel Mott was. Fifteen years later, piecing together my research and conference notes about shell shock, the penny began to drop. My Uncle Louis had been a patient of a 'thin, dark man with the abrupt manner', the practitioner of faradism, Colonel Frederick Mott.

Former greenhouses in the Crichton grounds. At one point my Uncle Louis was a gardener at the Crichton

REFERENCES

[1] *Owen, W (1920) 'Mental Cases' in Poems. London: Chatto and Windus.*
[2] *Winter, J (2000) 'Shell Shock and the Cultural History of the Great War', Journal of Contemporary History, 35 (1) pp 7–11.*
[3] *Kenyon, K, La Piana, FG, and Appleton, B (1979) 'Ocular malingering and hysteria: diagnosis and management', Survey of Ophthalmology, 24 (2) pp 89–96.*

[4] Slobodin R (1978) *WHR Rivers: Pioneer Anthropologist, Psychiatrist of the Ghost Road.* New York City: Columbia University Press.

[5] Myers, CS (1915) 'A contribution to the study of shell shock', *The Lancet,* 185 (4) 4772, 13 pp 316–20.

[6] Alexander, F (1987) *Psychosomatic medicine.* London: WW Norton & Co Inc.

[7] Brook, A, Elder A, and Zalidis S (1998) 'Psychological aspects of eye disorders', *Journal of the Royal Society of Medicine,* 91 pp 270–2.

[8] Johns, J (1998) 'The William Inman Trust'. The mind's eye, *Psychoanal. Psychotherapy,* 12 (2) pp 121–3.

[9] Balint, M (1986) *The Doctor, his Patients and the Illness.* London: Pitman Publishing Ltd.

[10] Brook, A and Fenton, P (1994) 'Psychological aspects of disorders of the eye: a pilot research project', *Psych. Bulletin,* 18 pp 135–7.

[11] Freud, S and Holden W (1998) *Shell Shock: the Psychological Impact of War.* London: Macmillan Publishers Ltd.

[12] Middleton, EM (1998) 'The mind's eye: psychological aspects of eye disorders', *Psychoanal. Psychotherapy,* 12 (2) pp. pp 148–9.

[13] Middleton, EM, Sinason, MDA, and Davids, Z (2007) 'Blurred vision due to psychosocial difficulties: a case series', *Eye,* 1–2 pp 316–7.

[14] Middleton, Sinason, and Davids. (2007) (2007) 'Blurred vision due to psychosocial difficulties: a case series', *Eye,* 1–2 pp 316–7.

[15] Freud, S (1920) 'Memorandum on the electrical treatment of war neurotics', *International Journal of Psychoanalysis,* 37 pp 16–18.

[16] Pow, T (2008) 'Charcot, Master of Saltpetriere, delivers his "Tuesday lecture" at the Crichton' in *Dear Alice. Narratives of Madness.* Cambridge: Salt Publishing.

[17] Shephard, B (2002) *War of Nerves: Soldiers and Psychiatrists 1914–1994.* London: Pimlico.

[18] Babington, A (1997) *Shell Shock: A History of the Changing Attitudes to War Neurosis.* Barnsley: Leo Cooper.

[19] Irvine, EF (1963) *A Pioneer of the New Psychology: Hugh Crichton-Miller.* Chatham: W & J Mackay & Co. Ltd.

[20] Macdonell, AG (1934) *England, Their England.* London: Macmillan in Slobodin, R (1978) *WHR Rivers: Pioneer Anthropologist, Psychiatrist of the Ghost Road.* New York City: Columbia University.

[21] Sassoon, S (1936) *Sherston's Progress*. London: Faber & Faber.

[22] Culpin, M (1949) 'An autobiography', *Occupational Psychology*, 23, 145 in Barham, P (2004) *Forgotten Lunatics of the Great War*. New Haven & London: Yale University Press.

[23] Jones, E (2014) 'An atmosphere of cure: Frederick Mott, shell shock and the Maudsley,' *History of Psychiatry*, 25 (4) pp 412-21.
Psychiatry, 25 (4) pp 412–21.

[24] Shephard (2002)

[25] Jones (2014) pp 412–21.

[26] Jones (2014) pp 412–21.

[27] Freud (1920) pp 16–18.

[28] Jones (2014) pp 412–21.

[29] Jones (2014) pp 412–21.

[30] Grogan, S (2014) *Shell Shocked Britain: the First World War's Legacy for Britain's Mental Health*. Barnsley: Pen & Sword Books Ltd.

[31] Grogan (2014)

[32] Freud (1920) pp 16–18.

[33] Shephard (2002)

[34] Yealland, LR (1918) *Hysterical Disorders of Warfare*. London: Macmillan & Co. in Shephard (2002)

[35] Shephard (2002)

[36] Adrian, ED (1919) 'Freud without tears' (unpublished talk) in Shephard (2002)

[37] Sayers, DL (1928) *The Unpleasantness at the Bellona Club*. London: Ernest Benn Ltd.

[38] Middleton, L (4 July 1916) Letter from Louis Middleton to his parents before sailing to France.

CHAPTER 4

WHAT'S IN A NAME?: LOUIS

Princess Louise, Duchess of Argyll, artist, feminist and social reformer (1848-1939)

Towards the end of the nineteenth century, Aberdeenshire *loons* were called Willie, Charlie, Sandy and the like. To coin a Billy Connolly song, *they werenae ca'ed* Louis.[1] So how did this regal, Gallic-sounding name rock up to this rural Aberdeenshire family? Not once – but twice! There are two likely sources.

Firstly, Uncle Louis Middleton's father (my grandfather) James Middleton, was a *lad o' pairts*. As a beneficiary of the nineteenth-century Scottish public (in the sense of non-fee paying and with open access) generalist educational system, he was a scholarship boy. Hailing from a modest Donside croft, this grandfather I never knew eventually went to Aberdeen University to study medicine. Instead of *mucking the byre* (cleaning out the cowshed) and helping with the *hairst* (harvest) he would be found behind the *stooks* (stacks of straw), poring over books, his reading matter brought in well-trodden fashion by the local *kirk* (church) minister.

As well as a man of medical science, James Middleton was a literary man and a devotee of his contemporary and compatriot, Robert Louis Stevenson (1850–94). Stevenson was known to his family and friends as Louis. I am fortunate to have inherited my grandfather's R L Stevenson library, including the Edinburgh edition of his works, and a bust of the author by the Scottish sculptor Henry Snell Gamley.

It is impossible to over-estimate Stevenson's influence on our family. Grandfather Middleton's admiration for his writing percolated down the generations. The *Kidnapped*[2] narrative framed my childhood, my father embellishing our lives with oft-quoted lines, a favourite being 'Am I no' a bonny fechter' – words from the novel's hunted Jacobite, Alan Breck. When visiting relatives in Edinburgh, I would pass over the Forth Rail Bridge with my dad to South Queensferry, a location that features in *Kidnapped*. I felt located in the myths of the Scottish imagination and in Scotland's troubled history. Fiction and fancy weave in and out of fact in Scottish culture; it is not always altogether clear which is which. With a formerly Catholic mother and a Presbyterian father, I was well placed to feel a resonance with Scotland's bipolar past, the backdrop to the novel. As a girl on holiday in the West Highlands, I could conjure up the image of Stevenson's kilt-clad Jacobite dashing through the heather. The reality for these blighted Highlanders, as I was later to discover, was a lot less romantic. It could be argued that their lot was systematic ethnic cleansing – but that is a theme for another book.[3]

Bust of R L Stevenson by H S Gamley, which belonged to my grandfather, Dr James Middleton

It seems pertinent to highlight a few aspects of the life of Robert Louis Stevenson, in order to understand the impact he had on my family in the choice of boys' names and possibly their attitude to war, and how the more worldly Stevenson may have influenced difficult life choices at challenging Middleton family times. In the days before television and social media, people were more influenced by what they read in books. So, dear reader, please indulge a consideration of the life of a fourth young Scotsman, Robert Louis Stevenson, this Scot of some considerable literary repute.

AN ORIGINAL SCOTTISH BOHEMIAN

Alas, like that other greatly loved Scots *scriever* Robert Burns, the life of the black-velvet-coated bohemian's life was cut tragically short. Burns' life had been snatched away a century earlier at the age of thirty-seven. Robert Louis Stevenson's life ended, suddenly and tragically in December 1894. He was forty-five and at the peak of his literary powers.

Stevenson had suffered poor health throughout his short life and the romantic writer had fatalistically anticipated dying young. Nevertheless, his premature death, thought to be a stroke following a lifetime of respiratory disease (believed at the time to be tuberculosis, though that is now questioned) would have greatly troubled my medical grandfather Middleton. Before the advent of vaccination and antibiotics, tuberculosis devastated families and rendered medical professionals helpless against that thief of young lives.

But, as with Burns, modern medical science is unclear about the cause of Stevenson's chronic ill health and early demise. Without the benefit of modern diagnostic techniques and pathology it is difficult to be sure. Little Lewis (as he was called at the time; he later changed his name to Louis) seems to have suffered in some ways a tortured but otherwise comfortable childhood. He was the sickly, only child of hypochondriacal parents and a complicated family dynamic. His father had also been over-protective of his wife's health. (After Stevenson's father's death, however, his widowed mother became an intrepid traveller, sailing to the South Seas in her son's entourage.) The child Lewis had been terrorised by his Calvinist nurse, Cummy, with her blood-curdling tales of hellfire and damnation. There was, in this family hothouse, a whiff of Munchausen's. Little Lewis suffered croup and an assortment of childhood ailments. In later life he suffered debilitating fits of coughing and, terrifyingly, especially to his highly anxious wife, Fanny, haemorrhaging. 'I have been spitting blood for a week.' [4]

The emerging Edinburgh writer, scion of the 'lighthouse Stevensons' who had shone a light on the seas around the land, struggled in vain to assert his burgeoning creative impulses in the face of paternal opposition. Young Louis was torn between filial duty to support his father in the successful family engineering business and his simultaneous longing to write. He was worn down by the conflict with his father. He did not want to follow in the family lighthouse footsteps but acquiesced as the dutiful son, and his health duly suffered.

Robert Louis Stevenson entered into what was for him an uncongenial university engineering environment and apprenticeship. Unlike Robert Burns, this effete Edinburgh man of letters was no ploughman poet and didn't fit in with the 'hardy sons of rustic toil'[5] who peopled Edinburgh University's engineering faculty. These industrious young men worked on the land to support themselves through their studies. Coastal highland trips on family lighthouse business with his father, however, fired the young man's romantic imagination; recollections were filed away for future reference, especially for his novel *Kidnapped*. The agnostic son's disavowal of Christianity was ultimately intolerable however to old man Stevenson and caused an even greater commotion in the Heriot Row household. Stevenson's mother had been a daughter of the manse, her father a minister in the Kirk. The family firm was ill-judged in forcing young Stevenson to follow suit.

The theme of the overbearing Victorian *paterfamilias* reverberated throughout my family too, amongst the Middletons, Forbes and the Thomsons. A medical future was mapped out for my uncle, young Louis Middleton. The plan had been that he follow grandfather Middleton into his medical practice in Peterhead. (Catastrophically he chose instead to go to war instead of completing his medical studies.) One wonders how much constrained, predictable lives, long before the days of package tour foreign holidays and gap years, facilitated the call to arms to young men seeking adventure. Old man Forbes considered a stint in the North of Scotland Bank – since absorbed by the Clydesdale Bank, and more recently merged with Virgin Money – to be suitable financial training for young farmer James (my great-uncle) and his older fledging farmer siblings, including my grandfather, Charles Forbes. It is entirely possible however that such pen-pushing would have been torture to these young farmers. It is not clear, moreover, what ultimately caused the falling out between Louis Thomson, my grandmother's cousin, and his apparently adoptive father, Uncle Willie, but the consequence was that this young Louis left the UK for France, at the end of the first decade of the twentieth century, never to live on this side of the Channel again. Freedom of expression and finding oneself would not seem then to have been the order of the day.

Skerryvore Lighthouse, designed by Alan Stevenson

Robert Stevenson (1772 –1850) had been one of Scotland's most accomplished civil engineers, acclaimed as one of the world's greatest lighthouse builders. His son - Louis' Uncle Alan however - had other ideas. Alan Stevenson had a religious calling and wanted to enter the

Kirk, but he was pressurised by his father into joining the family business. Nevertheless he went on to become an outstanding engineer, designing Scotland's tallest and most elegant lighthouse, Skerryvore, south-west of Tiree, on the all-important trade route to North America.

This career route had a high price: Alan suffered a severe breakdown in 1852 from which he never recovered. Louis' father, Thomas Stevenson, would then have felt even more in need of his son's support, so adding to the weight of expectation on young Louis' delicate shoulders. While many a grateful seafarer had been guided on his way by the work of these innovatory lighthouse designers, these engineers were unable to shine a reflective light upon themselves. It must have been obvious to most that the long-haired literary Louis was not engineering material.

Robert Louis Stevenson's conflicted existence and frustrated creative energies gradually wore away at him and he descended into depression. He agreed to study law by way of a compromise with his father, but he no more wanted to be an Edinburgh lawyer than a lighthouse engineer. Fortunately, outside help was at hand: aged twenty-three, young Louis was 'ordered south'[6] by an astute London-based Scots doctor, Andrew Clark (alumnus of Dundee High School and Aberdeen University), who cannily deduced the aetiology of his patient's debility. Dr Clark, an eminent chest physician, surmised it was not respiratory trouble that was ailing the lad (although Louis' lungs were susceptible), but the burden of familial expectations weighing down on him and impeding his career in writing. 'Clark is a trump'[7] Louis wrote to his friend Mrs Sitwell, who had referred him to the good doctor. Dr Clark's prescription of choice was a solitary dose of the Côte d'Azur and so Stevenson travelled south to Menton – where Louis Middleton was to arrive nearly half a century later as a shell shocked subaltern.

ORDERED SOUTH[8]

Menton, cette terre promise pour les poitrinaires de toute l'Europe [9]
(Menton, Europe's respiratory patients' promised land)

In Menton, Stevenson's Riviera destination, the belief is that he contracted tuberculosis while he was exiled there. The town at the time was popular with wealthy northern Europeans suffering from tuberculosis and requiring sanatorium care. When I visited Menton in 2016, local historian and Stevenson researcher, Jean Claude Volpi, outlined that he believed Stevenson resolved to be a professional writer during his sojourn there.

Later in life, Stevenson's doctors, including Clark, were inconclusive about the cause of his eventual chronic respiratory troubles. More recently, various theories suggest reasons other than tuberculosis for his ill-health, such as syphilis (common in the nineteenth century), bronchiectasis, or haemorrhagic telangiectasia (Osler-Rendu-Weber Syndrome), a hereditary disorder that can cause problems with the blood supply to the lungs.[10]

Nothing can change the eternal magnificence of form of the naked Alps behind Mentone.[11]

View of Menton from Cap Martin, Claude Monet

In any event, the hard-living Scot was immune to pleas from his medical advisers to improve his lifestyle by drinking less.[12] In 1880, Davos lung specialist Dr Karl Ruedi warned Stevenson off cigarettes, but the *bon viveur* took no heed of this advice then or later: '… as myself who has yet been obliged to strip himself, one after another, of all the pleasures that he had chosen except smoking (and the days of that I know in my heart ought to be over).' [13]

According to journalist Alexander Japp, when visiting Stevenson in Braemar (where the author began *Treasure Island* in 1881, and named characters after locals like John Silver, a meal miller) 'he … could fix you with his glittering e'e, and he would, as he points his sentences with a thin white forefinger, when this is not monopolised with his almost incessant cigarette.' This makes for painful reading in the light of contemporary knowledge about the damage caused by smoking.[14] Neither would cold, coal-burning *Auld Reekie* have been conducive to respiratory health, in spite of Edinburgh being the great medical centre of the day. Furthermore, granite dust from the family's lighthouse works possibly didn't help either and may have triggered silicosis. In any event Robert Louis Stevenson sadly died on 3 December 1894 in Vailima, his last home in the South Seas.

The granite villa at Glenshee Road, Braemar, with a plaque outlining it was where Robert Louis Stevenson wrote Treasure Island

THE NAMESAKE

A year after Stevenson's sudden, tragic death, my Middleton grandparents' first child was born – and the boy was named Louis. His father, my doctor grandfather, would have been devastated by the death of his hero Robert Louis Stevenson, and would have wanted to honour the great storyteller in a meaningful way.

John (my father, left) and Louis Middleton

LOUIS II

Secondly, family precedent would have influenced my grandparents, James and Mary Middleton, in their unusual choice of the name 'Louis' for their first-born son: my grandmother's cousin was also unusually named Louis. The older Louis was the regal-sounding Louis Léopold

Arthur William Thomson. He was christened thus, in spite of ostensibly coming from a modest highland family. So who was Louis Léopold Arthur William Thomson? And why was he so named?

Louis Thomson lived in Lancaster Gate, west London (not a mile from where I now live), initially at Laburnum Cottage, in the grounds of Kensington Palace (the cottage no longer exists) and subsequently at 2 Craven Terrace, Paddington.

My great-grandmother's brothers at the funeral of their young brother, James, 1865. Willie Thomson, Louis Thomson's apparent adoptive father, is in the centre at the back. To his left is Bruce Thomson's grandfather, Albert, one of the postmasters at Crathie, (and who reminds me of my father), and next left Alexander Thomson, Clerk-of-Works at Osborne House. Bruce Thomson is now the only remaining Thomson at Crathie, dwelling at the peerlessly situated Knock Art Gallery © Bruce Thomson

2 Craven Terrace, Paddington, London

Young Louis married on 14 November 1906 in Lancaster Gate Christ Church. (Apart from the spire, the original church no longer survives, apparently having suffered dry rot.) Louis' wife, Jeanne Marie Gabrielle Bordelais, was French, like his mother, Aunt Marie. Aunt Jeannie, as she came to be known by Crathie resident, Bruce Thomson, came from Nantes on the west coast of France. I have a connection with Nantes, my first port of call in France, where I went to stay with family friends, the Laffiché family. Christiane, Madame Laffiché, was present in Aberdeen when my parents met at their friends' wedding. One of Christiane's daughters, who became my good friend, Sylvaine, later worked as an archivist, and made a valuable connection for me with Jean-Claude Volpi, the local historian in Roquebrune-Cap Martin, who was to prove invaluable in developing my tale.

THE THOMSONS OF CRATHIE POST OFFICE

The Old Post Office, Crathie

What was cousin Louis Thomson's relationship to Uncle Louis Middleton? Both were descendants of the Thomsons of Crathie Post Office. My great-grandmother was Elizabeth Heslop, née Thomson. She was a sister of Willie Thomson, in the middle of the photograph of the Thomson clan brothers. Uncle Louis (Middleton's) mother, my grandmother, was a first cousin of Louis Thomson. To avoid confusion, I shall henceforth refer to Louis Middleton as Uncle Louis, and Louis Thomson as cousin Louis (although I would have called him Uncle Louis in real life, should I have known him. Such was the way in my family. That is why I refer to all these three First World War family men as 'my uncles in the Great War').

Elizabeth Heslop, née Thomson, my great-grandmother

My great-grandmother and her siblings were natives of Crathie, which is scenically situated above the mighty River Dee, the setting overlooking Balmoral Castle, with Crathie facing the darkly magnificent Lochnagar. The boys – contemporaries of Queen Victoria's favourite, John Brown – worked in royal service as foresters, porters, stable boys and the like at the local employer, Balmoral Castle. Queen Victoria refers to the Thomsons in her Highland Journals.[15]

At quarter to four I drove, with Louise, Beatrice, and Lady Ely, to John Thomson the wood forester's house for the christening of their child, three weeks old. Here, in their little sitting-room, in front of the window stood a table covered with a white cloth, on which was placed a basin with water, a bible, and a paper with the certificate of the child's birth.

We stood on one side, and John Thomson in his Highland dress next the minister, who was opposite me at the head of the table. Barbara, his wife, stood next to him, with the baby in her arms, and then the old Thomsons and their unmarried daughter, the Donald Stewarts, Grants, and Victoria, Morgan and sister, and Brown.

The Falls of Muick, the Balmoral Estate, by Louis L A W Thomson
7 September, 1896

Queen Victoria was a frequent visitor to Crathie Post Office, forging a strong connection between the royal family and the Thomsons of Crathie. The first postmaster was Charles Thomson who had been head forester on the Balmoral estate. Following the introduction of Uniform Penny Postage in 1840, and realising that the village of Crathie needed a post office, he set to and established one. After Charles' death in 1887 his son Albert (Uncle Willie's brother), at the request of Queen Victoria, became the Crathie postmaster.

Queen Victoria's pony Sultan with her servant Andrew Thomson (Uncle Willie's brother) at Balmoral in 1870. The dogs are from left to right: Sharp, Friskie (Princess Louise's), Dacko and Corran (which belonged to Prince Alfred)

The Queen had a high regard for the Thomson family and she employed other brothers in the royal estate: Albert's brother, Uncle Willie, was 'ordered south' and appointed page at Kensington Palace. His brother Alexander was moved to Osborne House, on the Isle of Wight, which the Queen and Prince Albert bought in 1845. Uncle Willie and his French wife, Aunt Marie, went to live at Laburnum Cottage in Kensington Gardens, where my late father, John Middleton, would visit them. Uncle Willie was to become a firm favourite of Queen Victoria's artistic daughter Louise.

Princess Louise's sculpture of Queen Victoria, Kensington Palace

Princess Louise was a prominent local figure in west London at the time. As well as being an accomplished sculptor, Princess Louise was an active social reformer in Notting Hill, where I now live. She promoted education for girls, and set up a local hospital with large grounds for mothers and children. 'The hospital has gone through several incarnations and no longer exists. Part of the freehold land registered in 1925 as the Princess Louise Hospital, and St Quintin's Health Centre now houses the current Princess Louise of Kensington Nursing Home'.[16] Next door, on what was the same parcel of land, also lies St Quintin's Kitchen Garden, where I have a small raised bed.[17]

The author with French third cousin Jean Max Thomson (Louis Thomson's grandson) and his daughter, Adèle, outside the Princess Louise of Kensington Nursing Home, Pangbourne Avenue, London, 2016

When Louise's husband, John George Edward Henry Douglas Sutherland Campbell, the Marquess of Lorne (and future 9th Duke of Argyll) became Governor General of Canada, and the family moved to Ottawa, their entourage included Princess Louise's servant, Uncle Willie Thomson and his French wife Marie.

Uncle Willie and Aunt Marie went to Canada childless – but came home, surprisingly to their relations, with a baby called Louis. There had been no notice of pregnancy to the family. The dates within which to have a baby did not fit, according to my late father, John Middleton, and his late sister, my Auntie Maisie (Mary McKichan, who had been the children's nursing sister at Queen Mary's Hospital, in the East End, London). This assessment about Louis Thomson's birth concurs with that of Bruce Thomson, the only surviving Thomson at Crathie. As my father and aunt both delighted in surmising, Louis Thomson was Princess Louise's *merry-begotten* or lovechild, her illegitimate son.

It was said at the time and since, that Princess Louise's husband was homosexual, and that the princess had at least one love affair in Canada. Being in the royal realm, Lorne's homosexuality was not openly and publicly acknowledged; furthermore, homosexuality was a criminal offence at the time and likely to incur imprisonment. Lucinda Hawksley explores the subject of Lorne's sexuality in her book, *The mystery of Princess Louise: Queen Victoria's rebellious daughter*.[18] Suggestions about his proclivities date from his time at Eton when he was alleged to have featured unnamed in a known paedophile teacher's poem about his pupil's relationship with his friend, Frederick Wood. Lorne was later known to be associated with the gay underworld. There were documented references to his proclivities in 'the other direction'[19] and the future King Edward V11, perhaps more aware of Lorne's tendencies, was opposed to his sister's prospective union. Researchers such as Hawksley have been blocked from accessing the Duke of Argyll's archives for further documentary evidence.[20] One is tempted to think that the Campbells are sensitive to enquiries about their sexual peccadillos, having also lived through the infamous divorce of Ian Campbell, the 11th Duke of Argyll and Margaret, Duchess of Argyll, in the sixties.

Inveraray Castle, seat of Clan Campbell

There is some evidence however that the Canadians were querulous at the time about Princess Louise's lack of children, and seem to have asked knowing questions about their Governor General. In Wikipedia it is documented that Louise and Lorne 'shared a common love of the arts, but the marriage was childless and unhappy, and they spent much time apart. Lorne formed close friendships with men, including Lord Ronald Gower, Morton Fullerton, and the Count de Mauny, who were known to be homosexual or bisexual, which fuelled rumours in London society that he shared their proclivities.[21] Canadian writer, Sandra Gwyn, in writing about Canadian Governor Generals, states unequivocally in a chapter entitled 'The Gay Governor-General' that 'Lorne was, almost certainly, a homosexual, and not always one who remained in the closet'. She continues and confirms earlier speculation that: 'As a schoolboy at Eton, as the British scholar Timothy D'Arch Smith has revealed … he had been involved in a relationship with another sprig of the aristocracy, Frederick Wood, the future Lord Halifax… In later years, Lorne was well-known as an habitué of certain illicit London clubs and to attend what were discreetly described as "masculine parties" '.[22]

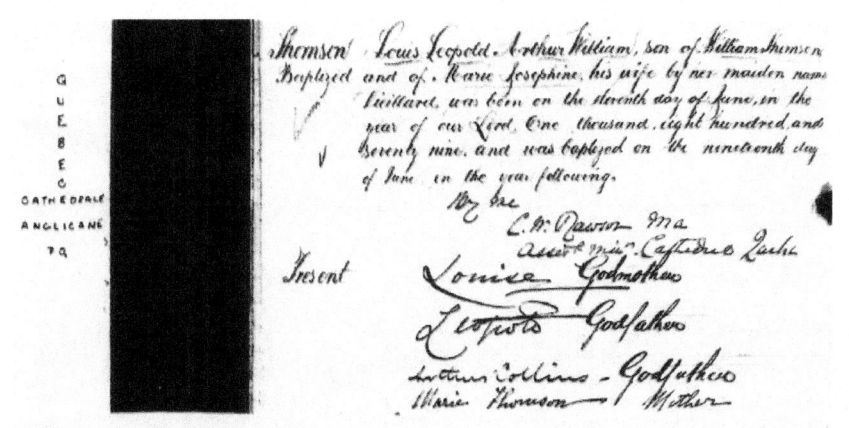

Louis Thomson's christening certificate, present were Princess Louise and Prince Leopold

And so in Canada the baby Louis Léopold Arthur William Thomson was born. His birth was dated 11 June 1879 and his christening certificate (above) a year later on 19 June 1880. I have been unable to trace a birth certificate. My lawyer cousin in Canada confirms there were no birth certificates issued at the time of Louis Thomson's birth in Canada. Had there been, and had it been available, it would have been interesting to see. Whatever the reason, Princess

Louise left Canada without her husband on 18 October 1879 for the United Kingdom, arriving in Liverpool on 30 October 1880. She returned to Canada on 3 February 1881. Passenger lists for their voyages were not documented. I have been unable to trace further the dates of the Atlantic comings and goings of the Thomson family.

For a child of ostensibly humble Highland origins, the christening witnesses and Godmother and Godfather are unusual: 'Louise' and 'Léopold' – that is Princess Louise and Prince Léopold, Queen Victoria's haemophiliac son. The choice of the child's name, Louis Léopold Arthur William, is etymologically interesting too, Louis reminiscent of Louise, and Léopold, not commonly the middle name of a son of a family from the glens. 'Inconvenient' royal children were sometimes adopted by servants, and in this case, according to my family oral history, by the hitherto childless Uncle Willie and Aunt Marie. Cousin Louis was to have no siblings.

The Mill at Inver by Louis Léopold Arthur William Thomson, 1896

Louis Thomson was not the only child with maternity attributed to Princes Louise. Lucinda Hawksley relates the tale of another illegitimate son. When I heard this author was to be presenting a local lecture where I live on the subject of Princess Louise's illegitimate son on 21 January 2014, I went along thinking it to be about my relation. Instead, I was to hear about how another baby was born to Princess Louise around the end of 1866 or early 1867, and was adopted by another medical family. The adoptive father, Frederick Locock, was the son of Sir Charles Locock, Queen Victoria's *accoucher* (the term at the time for obstetrician). And, as with my family, Princess Louise's parentage of the child Henry Locock was an accepted part of their family oral history.

Final resting place of Sir Charles Locock, Kensal Green Cemetery, west London

Young Louis was to grow up in Laburnum Cottage, Kensington Palace, and his benefactress, Princess Louise, financed him through medicine at St Mary's Hospital, Paddington, another matter-of-fact part of my family history. I have not been able to find documentation about this funding, in spite of extensive research in the family and making enquiries to the Royal Colleges. After graduation the young doctor worked as a general practitioner in Lewisham and made holiday trips to Crathie.

UK & Ireland Medical Directory 1925

He married French woman Jeanne Marie Gabrielle Bordelais (called Aunt Jeannie by Crathie-based Bruce Thomson) in 1906.

Marriage certificate of Louis Léopold Arthur William Thomson and Jeanne Marie Gabrielle Bordelais at Paddington, London, 1906

Dr Louis Thomson then moved to France, his adopted mother country, to spend his life as a country family doctor.

Dr Louis Léopold Arthur William Thomson late in life

REFERENCES

1 Connolly, B *(1974) Cop yer whack for this. UK: Polydor.*
2 Stevenson, RL *(1886) Kidnapped. London: Cassell & Co Ltd*
3 *After completion of this chapter, the Braemar Local History Group published a fascinating and sobering text, 'Jacobites and Upper Deeside', that outlined the tragic and brutal fate of the Jacobites.*
4 Stevenson, RL *(1883) Letter to his mother in Mehew, E (ed.) (1997) Selected Letters of Robert Louis Stevenson. New Haven and London: Yale University Press. pp 243-244*
5 Burns, R *(1786) The cotter's Saturday night in Harman C (2005). Robert Louis Stevenson: a Biography. London: HarperCollins Publishers.*
6 Stevenson, RL *(1909) 'Ordered South' in Virginibus Puerisque and Other Papers. London: Chatto & Windus.*
7 Stevenson, RL *(1883) Letter to Mrs Sitwell in Mehew, E. (ed.) (1997) p 52.*
8 Stevenson, RL *(1909)*
9 Volpi, J-C *Nice-Matin 7 November 2015*
10 Guttmacher AE & Callahan JR *(2000) 'Did Robert Louis Stevenson have hereditary hemorrhagic telangiectasia?' Am J Med Genet. 6:91 (1) pp 62–5.*
11 Stevenson, RL *(1909)*
12 Harman, C *(2005) Robert Louis Stevenson: a Biography. London: HarperCollinsPublishers*
13 Stevenson, RL *(1885) Letter to his William Archer in Mehew (1997). p 293.*
14 Japp A *(1905) Robert Louis Stevenson: A Record, an Estimate, and a Memorial. London: TW Laurie.*
15 Victoria, R *(1868) in Duff, D (ed.) (1994) Queen Victoria's Highland Journals. London: Reed Consumer Books Ltd.*
16 *https://ezitis.myzen.co.uk/princesslouise.html searched 23 November 2020.*
17 HM Land Registry *Current title plan Title number BGL3132.*
18 Hawksley, L *(2013) The mystery of Princess Louise: Queen Victoria's rebellious daughter. London: Chatto & Windus*
19 *Letter from H J Cavendish to M Gledhill in Hawksley, L (2013).*
20 Hawksley, L *(2013)*
21 Wikipedia *searched 25 March 2021.*
22 Gwyn, S *(1985) The Private Capital: Ambition and love in the age of Macdonald and Laurier in Hawksley, L (2013).*

CHAPTER 5

THE PATH TO CAP MARTIN

Cette péninsule bénie des dieux. Volpi, J-C [1]
This peninsula blessed by the gods.

Sentier au Cap Martin (Path to Cap Martin) Claude Monet, 1884

I happened upon another voice from the past in my late father's papers – an undated postcard sent by Dr Louis Thomson, then a doctor in the French army, to my grandparents. He wanted to meet his young cousin, Louis Middleton, in Cap Martin. I was intrigued. Where was Cap Martin? What on earth was my uncle, the subaltern 2nd Lieutenant, my uncle Louis Middleton, doing there? When was this sent? And did the two Louis-s meet? A scenic trail was opened up in my search for these enigmatic family men.

And this picturesque destination, I discovered to my joy, had been painted by the great French Impressionist, Clause Monet, in April 1884.

Postcard from cousin Louis Thomson to my grandparents

Some investigations, including enquiries to the Gordon Highlanders' Museum and an email to Jean-Max Thomson (Louis Thomson's grandson in Toulouse) guided me to the path to Cap Martin. Although Louis Thomson's postcard was undated, according to Jean-Max and his mother, Madame Aline Thomson (Louis Thomson's daughter-in-law) the ages of his children on the reverse point to it having been sent between November 1918 and March 1919. But what was Louis Middleton doing there in the French Riviera at the end of the war and did those two medical cousins manage to have a rendezvous in Cap Martin? Those questions intrigued me.

I had never heard of Cap Martin. No-one in our Broughty Ferry home had ever mentioned it to me. In fact, the first and only time our family went abroad - to Alassio, a scenic Italian town only a few kilometres along this glorious Mediterranean coast – no mention was made of Cap Martin, although my parents took a day trip to nearby

Monte Carlo. (Monaco is on the other side of the bay from Cap Martin.) Had my father known of his brother's stay in Cap Martin, I feel pretty sure there would have been a quiet emotional resonance, and possibly an effort to visit the place where his brother had been on his own, but this doesn't appear have been the case. I don't think my father ever knew his brother had been there. Being a schoolboy at the time of the First World War, I doubt my father would have known the details of his older brother's sojourn on the Côte d'Azur.

CAP MARTIN

Cap Martin is less well known than the other glamorous Côte d'Azur headlands – Cap Ferrat, Cap Antibes and Cap d'Ail – perhaps because it had historically been under private ownership. It belonged for centuries to the Grimaldi family, who had hunted in this uncultivated peninsula of aromatic pines. Two millennia previously, Cap Martin was the homeland of the Mantoni tribe (hence *Menton* or the Italian *Mentone*); in Roman times it was invaded by Caesar Augustus and Roman remains – such as the Mausolée de Lumone on the old Via Julia Augusta (road to Rome) – may still be seen in the area.

Mausolée de Lumone, Roquebrune-Cap-Martin, a relic of Roman occupation

The peninsula's history becomes more relevant to our tale from the latter part of the nineteenth century, with the construction of le Grand Hôtel du Cap Martin.

LE GRAND HOTEL DU CAP MARTIN

Postcard of le Grand Hôtel du Cap Martin before the First World War

The Grand Hôtel du Cap Martin stands at the peak of the cape – and grand it certainly is. This palatial residence was perhaps the most spectacular of all the opulent hotels and exclusive residences and villas scattered around the Menton area. The Grand Hotel commands an elevated position on the tip of the headland, skirted by dazzling white limestone rocks. Surveying all around, the hotel's view extends from the incongruous high-rise buildings of Monte Carlo to the west, and to Italy in the east, with the backdrop of the glorious Alpes Maritimes. Below flow the azure waters of the Mediterranean.

Chalk-white rocks at Cap Martin, facing the skyscrapers of Monaco

Situated just across the bay from Monte Carlo, the Cap Martin Hotel attracted the rich and elite of the day. Closer by is the neighbouring *commune* of Menton (or Mentone). This Italianate town was historically disputed between France and Italy and is now in French hands. Menton is a short walk from the hotel: Cap Martin is just a couple of hundred metres from the boundary between the two towns Roquebrune-Cap-Martin and Menton. The setting of the hotel is certainly spectacular. The words of Robert Louis Stevenson come to mind: 'Nothing can change the eternal magnificence of form of the naked Alps behind Mentone.' [1]

Just as Stevenson had inspired the Middletons pre-war, the question of the writer's influence comes to mind again here. Did Robert Louis Stevenson's recuperative trip to nearby Menton suggest the choice of location for Louis Middleton's convalescence? Was Louis Middleton, like Robert Louis Stevenson, 'ordered south'?

Although it is not clear to me how much influence my family would have had or how much decision-making lay with the military authorities, the family would have struggled to know what to do about their severely shell shocked son at the end of the war. Psychological medicine, as outlined in earlier chapters, was in its infancy. General practitioner, Dr Middleton, would have been as much at sea as anyone else with the mental malaise of his oldest son. Ever the Stevenson-scholar, my grandfather would have been aware of the Menton location of his writer-hero's convalescence from depression in 1873. I have inherited my grandfather's copy of *Virginibus Puerisque and other papers*. In it is 'Ordered south', Stevenson's musings about his stay on the Côte d'Azur.[2][3][4]

I doubt, though, whether Dr Middleton would have been aware of Stevenson's more colourful antics there, including self-medication. In 1873–4, the writer headed one day to the gaming tables of the nearby Monte Carlo with his friend and mentor, Sidney Colvin. The black-velvet-jacketed Stevenson was denied entry to the casino on account of his bohemian appearance. He also frequented the opium dens of Garavan, an eastern suburb of Menton near the Italian border.[5] One wonders how these intoxicating experiences fed the already florid imagination of the author of *Dr Jekyll and Mr Hyde*. So my question here is, was Louis Middleton 'ordered south' into Stevenson's erstwhile Riviera retreat?

THE GRAND HOTEL
AND THE FIRST WORLD WAR

The Michelham Convalescent Home No 8

How did the Grand Hotel, this magnificent palace, haunt of the European elite, the rich and famous, become a convalescent home for British officers? The spectacular *belle époque* edifice was given over to the war effort by wealthy British ex-patriots in the Riviera. But why here, so far from the mud of the Somme from whence many of the war-weary trudged? Even in 2016, the journey was long, and took half a day from the north of France to Cap Martin. In the pre-TGV trains of nearly a century ago, it would have been much slower, and the battle-weary former combatants would not have been buoyed up for the rigours of a long journey. On addressing this to local Roquebrune-Cap-Martin historian, Jean-Claude Volpi, in 2016, he said of the journey of a century ago, *c'etait facile* – the journey was easy.

So how did this opulent convalescent home come into being – and in such an exotic setting? The Côte d'Azur had long attracted wealthy northern Europeans, especially writers, artists, and the sick. As far back as 1766 the Scottish surgeon Tobias Smollett had put nearby Nice on the British map with his *Travels through France and Italy*[6] –

although not always flatteringly. Nice lies 18 miles [29 km] west of Menton.

THE FRENCH RIVIERA

Smollett, a self-confessed malcontent, first wrote disparagingly about Provence. He grumbled about the 'garlic-smelling workers, who spent all their time sitting in the sun', and groused about the food, the 'cold, dismal and dirty' inns, the 'lazy, greedy, and impertinent' coachmen and so on. With time he was eventually won over by the light and delights of Provence - the temperate climate, the picturesque scenery – and the food. The wines eventually won his approval, too, being 'very nearly as good as Burgundy'! So much was the surgeon ultimately charmed that he applied to be British consul to Nice, but the British foreign minister declined Smollett's offer, fearing a backlash to his earlier negativity.

A century after Smollett, another British medic established Menton as a therapeutic centre. Mancunian Dr James Henry Bennet had suffered from tuberculosis and had apparently recovered in Menton. Bennet attributed his own return to health to the congenial climate. Following the publication of an article in *The Lancet*[7] in 1860 and his books *Winter and Spring on the Shores of the Mediterranean*[8] and *Mentone and the Riviera as a Winter Climate*[9], wealthy northern European consumptives coughed and spluttered their way south on the recently opened steam railway, the P L M (Paris-Lyon-Méditerranée).

Postcard extolling the convenience of the P L M railroad

Sadly, the confinement of hundreds of infectious patients in the carriages, the temperate climate on arrival and minimal nineteenth-century public health provision did little to help those with chest infections. Indeed – according to local historian, Monsieur Jean-Claude Volpi – it is thought locally that, in spite of a lifetime of ill-health, and having been 'ordered south'[10] to Menton for health reasons, Robert Louis Stevenson had actually contracted tuberculosis in Menton. Stevenson became a patient of Dr Bennet, who agreed with Stevenson's friend and doctor in London, Dr Clark, that the writer was depressive, not consumptive. Stevenson's letters from Menton in late 1873 would appear to support this view.[11]

Postcard advertising Menton hotels

Nevertheless, the grand hotels grew and flourished, with names such as Victoria, Balmoral and the Winter Palace reflecting the clientele. The area became established as a sanatorium for wealthy northern Europeans, attracting both respiratory patients and winter escapees, especially from Britain and Russia, until the tsunami of the Great War convulsed the continent.

Hôtel Prince de Galles, Menton

Situated on the Menton seafront, the Hôtel Prince de Galles was one of Robert Louis Stevenson's abodes during 1873–4. Curiously, there is no placard acknowledging his stay there or anywhere else in Menton, although there is much local acknowledgement of onetime Menton resident, the New Zealand writer, Katherine Mansfield.

But perhaps the grandest of all the local hotels was the Grand Hôtel du Cap Martin.

Le Grand Hôtel du Cap Martin, 1907

The land on which this palatial hotel stands had been bought by Scotsman George Calvin White along with a consortium of British, French, Belgians and Americans in 1889, and the hotel was built in 1891.[12] Not long before the hotel was built, the great French Impressionist painter, Claude Monet, painted a series of paintings on and around Cap Martin, in April 1884. These are now in the public domain and feature on postcards to be found in the locality.

One of Claude Monet's series of Cap Martin paintings, 1884

White commissioned Danish architect Hans-Georg Tersling to design the building to a high specification. Tersling, who had started life as a carpenter, was a graduate of Copenhagen's prestigious Royal Danish Academy of Fine Arts and became one of the most prolific *belle époque* architects. He drew on the neoclassical Louis XVI style and was also inspired by the Italian Renaissance. Herr Tersling also designed the *grande salle* of the casino at Monte Carlo as well as the casino in Menton and a number of other lavish Riviera villas.

Opened in 1891,[2] the Grand Hôtel du Cap Martin became an exclusive holiday haunt for European royalty and aristocracy, as well as the social and political elite of the day. Guests included Queen Victoria, her daughters Victoria and Maud, the future Edward VII and the future George V, Empress Eugenie, wife of Napoleon III, Prince Napoleon Charles Bonaparte, Emperor Franz Joseph and Elisabeth (Sissi), future Empress of Austria and campaigner for improved conditions for the mentally ill, as well as countless other European royals. Sissi is held in high regard locally.

Memorial plaque to 'Sissi', Elisabeth, Empress of Austria, on Menton esplanade

Political visitors included William Gladstone and his wife in 1895 and David Lloyd George in 1910. The sculptor Auguste Rodin, who was a friend of Robert Louis Stevenson, was another of the hotel's illustrious guests. Among the grand dukes, barons, counts and bankers who visited the hotel in 1903 was Glaswegian grocer and tea magnate, Sir Thomas Lipton, his brand of tea responsible still for many an overseas brew, from Cannes to Kolkata. One 1911 visitor never to return was Archduke Franz Ferdinand of Austria, who was assassinated in Sarajevo on 28 June 1914.[13][14]

With the ensuing advent of the First World War the local tourist industry was threatened, but, with an eye to the future, there was an effort to keep the Grand Hôtel going and to maintain its exclusivity. Wealthy British residents turned over other local grand hotels such as the Imperial to the war effort as hospitals for British and French soldiers. British merchant banker Lord Michelham and his wife negotiated with the owners of the Grand Hôtel du Cap Martin to do likewise. It was agreed that, in association with the Red Cross, it could become a convalescent home for British and Canadian officers – the Michelham Convalescent Home No 8.[15][16]

Recuperating residents at the Cap Martin Hotel included Ford Madox Ford, author of *Parade's End*, and Scots-Canadian surgeon John McCrae. In the words of the convalescent Ford:

> ... *but we had lived like gentlemen in that Red Cross Hôtel on Cap Martin. A peeress of untellable wealth and inexhaustible benevolence had taken us for chest sufferers of H M Army ... for us alone all the Hôtel Cap Martin ... One of those great gilded caravanserais that of my own motion I should never have entered. We had at our disposal staff, kitchens, chef – and a great chef of before the days when Anglo-Saxondom had ruined these shores – wine-cellars, riding-horses, golf-course, automobiles ...*
>
> *We had sat at little tables in fantastically palmed and flowering rooms and looked from the shadows of marble walls over a Mediterranean that blazed in the winter sunlight. We ate Tournedos Meyerbeer and drank Château Pavie 1906 ... 1906, think of that.*
>
> *We slept in royal suites; the most lovely ladies and the most nobly titled elderly seigneurs walked with us on the terraces over the sea. Sometimes one looked round and remembered for a second that we were all being fattened for slaughter.* [17]

One of those great gilded caravanserais Ford Madox Ford

In 1916, Scots-Canadian poet and physician John McCrae was recovering at the Grand Hôtel from pleurisy. He had been horrified by the use of chlorine gas at Ypres. When a friend of his was killed in action on 2 May 1915 – six weeks before the death there of my great uncle James Forbes – McCrae was transfixed by the blood-red poppies growing among the little crosses that marked makeshift graves. The next day he wrote:[18]

In Flanders fields the poppies blow
Between the crosses, row on row,
That mark our place; and in the sky
The larks, still bravely singing, fly
Scarce heard amid the guns below.

We are the Dead. Short days ago
We lived, felt dawn, saw sunset glow,
Loved and were loved, and now we lie
In Flanders fields.

Take up our quarrel with the foe:
To you from failing hands we throw
The torch; be yours to hold it high.
If ye break faith with us who die
We shall not sleep, though poppies grow
In Flanders fields.

Little could McCrae have imagined the potency his poppies would accrue.

'Blood Swept Lands and Seas of Red': art installation of ceramic poppies at the Tower of London, marking 100 years since the start of the Great War

LOST IN PARADISE

According to local Roquebrune historian Jean-Claude Volpi, author of *Le Cap Martin, Entre Monte-Carlo et Menton*,[19] only purely convalescing officers were to be accepted at the Grand Hotel and those who were wounded, infectious or ill were barred. The price of the exclusivity of this location was high. My Uncle Louis Middleton was gravely ill, but in spite of the prohibition against sick residents, he would have been sent to this exotic location with the best of intentions. The idyllic surroundings, the physical comfort and the cuisine were superlative in this favoured haunt of nobility. This quiet, psychologically broken young man 'ordered south' from the worst battlefield in British history, would have been aware of the privilege and would have suffered in silence. He would have contained his horror, his companion nightmares. The probability was that my uncle would have had limited, if any, opportunity to address his nocturnal hauntings with skilled professional help. He would have been lost. As discussed elsewhere in these pages, the understanding of shell shock was in its infancy; it was a question of luck whether or not one arrived at an appropriately therapeutic haven.

The Grand Hôtel du Cap Martin early in the 21st century, now a gated community of exclusive apartments owned mostly by Russians

For the casualties of the First World War, in this case the shell shocked subaltern, was any respite whatsoever to be had in this scenic Mediterranean destination and playground of the rich? Would the magnificence of the Riviera setting, 'the sea and the pines'[20] and the opulence of the Grand Hôtel du Cap Martin make soothing inroads into the 'haunted nightly'[21]?

An answer may be considered by the outcome of my uncle's life: After his sojourn by the azure waters of the Mediterranean, he spent the next and last fifty years of his life in a psychiatric institution.

Contemporary entrance to the Grand Hôtel du Cap Martin

RENDEZVOUS AT CAP MARTIN?

Do we know if Dr Louis Thomson, the third relation in this tale of war, visited his younger cousin and namesake Louis Middleton at Cap Martin? If he had, how would the elder Louis, the experienced war doctor, have influenced the care of his broken-down younger cousin, if at all? After extensive enquiries I have been unable to find any record of their having met, neither familial, medical nor military. The Red Cross destroyed case notes at the end of the war, as did the military medical authorities. But knowing my family, the probability I wager is that these two young medical men would have met.

One of Cousin Louis Thomson's grandchildren, Jean-Max Thomson, recounts, however, that Dr Thomson did not like the embryonic discipline of psychoanalysis, in spite of his intellectual wife being a friend of the writer Romain Rolland. Rolland had influenced Freud. Rolland created the notion of the 'oceanic feeling' (for example, as felt by fans in a football crowd or in certain other large group, religious or cult events). This was later adopted by Sigmund Freud. Rolland coined the phrase in a letter to Freud dated 5 December 1927:

> ... But I would have liked to see you doing an analysis of spontaneous religious sentiment or, more exactly, of religious feeling, which is ... the simple and direct fact of the feeling of the 'eternal' (which can very well not be eternal, but simply without perceptible limits, and like oceanic, as it were).[22]

The author 'looking for Louis', Menton

In his book *The Future of an Illusion*,[23] Freud ends with a discussion of the oceanic concept, and picks it up again in *Civilization and Its Discontents*,[24] where he responds to Rolland's request. He doesn't acknowledge Rolland, but credits the concept to an anonymous friend.

Was any rehabilitative effect at all to be gained from staying in this idyllic spot? I leave it to no other than the scribe of the sick-bed, our old friend Robert Louis Stevenson, in a posting in 1883 during his melancholic sojourn in Menton:

> *He recognises with his intelligence that this thing and that thing is beautiful, while in his heart of hearts he has to confess that it is not beautiful for him. It is in vain that he spurs his discouraged spirit; in vain that he chooses out points of view, and stands there, looking with all his eyes, and waiting for some return of*

the pleasure that he remembers in other days, as the sick folk may have awaited the coming of the angel at the pool of Bethesda. He is like an enthusiast leading about with him a stolid, indifferent tourist. There is some one by who is out of sympathy with the scene, and is not moved up to the measure of the occasion; and that some one is himself. The world is disenchanted for him. He seems to himself to touch things with muffled hands, and to see them through a veil. His life becomes a palsied fumbling after notes that are silent when he has found and struck them. He cannot recognise that this phlegmatic and unimpressionable body with which he now goes burthened, is the same that he knew heretofore so quick and delicate and alive. [25]

IN LOUIS' FOOTSTEPS

The author at le Golfe Bleu 2016

In 2016 serendipity came my way when I was awarded a stay in Cabbé, which lies between Cap Martin and Monaco. 'Cabbé' was the old Mentonnais word for *Cap* or Cape. The setting was idyllic with a tropical allotment in a gully adjacent to our temporary home.

Le Vieux Moulin, with allotment below

The building at the other side of this vegetable garden is *le Vieux Moulin*, where the young officers from the Grand Hôtel ate at night.

Le Vieux Moulin, viewed from le Golfe Bleu

    According to Jean-Claude Volpi, word had got out a hundred years ago that a local woman, Madame Blanche Imbert from Cabbé, made a very good French dish of the day there.

Steps to le Vieux Moulin

*The author on the steps down to le Vieux Moulin, where her
Uncle Louis would have eaten*

These young Scotsmen, Englishmen and Canadians, freed from battlefield bully beef and hardtack biscuits, hot-footed it (or went by tram) to Cabbé in pursuit of the legendary meals and, I expect, company.

Old postcard of the era of the tram that linked Cap Martin to Cabbé

At the time the only two buildings on the whole headland were the *Grand Hôtel* and the *Vieux Moulin*. Dairy cattle that supplied the hotel with milk grazed on the scrubland between. Now there is a little snack bar on the site of the *Vieux Moulin*.

The author outside the Vieux Moulin

The last convoy of forty-nine convalescing officers arrived at the *Grand Hôtel* on 3 March 1919. Three weeks later it was shut to combatants in the presence of one of the earlier protagonists in our tale: Princess Louise, partial progenitor of the 'Louis' etymological root, officially closed the Michelham Convalescent Home No 8 on 25 March 1919.

The author on the beach in front of le Grand Hôtel du Cap Martin

During the course of the Great War the Grand Hôtel du Cap-Martin welcomed more than twelve hundred Scottish, English and Canadian officers. These young men would have had a memorable stay of two or three weeks in an exotic location on the Côte d'Azur. Sea bathing, French cuisine and fine wine, and the superbly appointed accommodation would have offered an almost unimaginable respite from the trenches and the bully beef. It is less clear, however, if this idyll would have offered relief to the 'haunted nightly'. Coming from the mud of the Somme and similar - and during the war knowing they were going back – would have, I imagine, clouded this scenic sojourn with a sense of unreality. I have no doubt that the Michelham Convalescent Home No 8 would have provided superb medical and nursing care. I have no information about the nature there of the psychological care, but fear it was most likely at best inadequate and more likely non-existent. As discussed elsewhere in these pages, appropriate treatment for the mental wounds of war was at that time in its infancy.

Le Grand Hôtel, now private apartments

REFERENCES

[1] Volpi, J-C *Le Cap Martin: Entre Monte-Carlo et Menton.* Menton: Imprimerie TTG.
[2] Stevenson, R L (1909) 'Ordered south' in *Virginibus Puerisque and other papers.* London: Chatto & Windus.
[3] Harman, C (2005) *Robert Louis Stevenson: a Biography.* London: Harper Collins Publishers.
[4] Mehew, E (ed.) (1997) *Selected Letters of Robert Louis Stevenson.* New Haven and London: Yale University Press.
[5] Balti, B (2012) *Voyage au Bout de l'Etrange.* Fouesnant: Yoran Embanner:
[6] Smollett, T G (1949) *Travels through France and Italy.* London: John Lehmann.
[7] Bennett, H B (1860) 'A winter at Mentone, near Nice.' *The Lancet,* 76 (1923) pp 2–5.
[8] Bennet, H B (1870) *Winter and Spring on the Shores of the Mediterranean.* New York: D Appleton and Co.
[9] Bennet, H B (1860) *Mentone and the Riviera as a Winter Climate.* London: John Churchill.
[10] Stevenson (1909)
[11] Mehew, E (ed.) (1997) *Selected letters of Robert Louis Stevenson.* New Haven and London: Yale University Press.
[12] Wright K (2016) *The Great War and the British on the French Riviera.* Kidderminster: Kwite Write Publishing.
[13] Volpi pp 15–22.
[14] Wright (2016) p 32.
[15] Volpi p 27.'
[16] Wright (2016) pp 33–7.
[17] Ford, M F (1938) *Revival: Provence from Minstrelsy to the Machine* Abingdon: Routledge Revivals.
[18] McCrae, J (1919) *In Flanders Fields.* New York and London: G P Putnam's Sons.
[19] Volpi, J-C.
[20] Stevenson (1909)
[21] Pow, T (2008) 'Glass' in 'Foucault: Two tales and a Bedlam ballad' in *Dear Alice. Narratives of Madness.* Cambridge: Salt Publishing.
[22] https://heteroglossia.tumblr.com/post/28983817406/your-analysis-of-religion-is-a-just-one-but-i. (Accessed 8 September 2021).
[23] Freud, S (1927) *The Future of an Illusion.* Eastford: Martino Fine Boo
[24] Freud, S (1929) *Civilisation and its Discontents* Eastford: Martino Fine Books.
[25] Stevenson (1909) pp 88.

CHAPTER 6

THE STUDENT SOLDIER

A Gordon for me, a Gordon for me,
If you're no' a Gordon, you're nae use to me,
The Black Watch are braw, the Seaforths an' a',
But the cocky wee Gordon's the pride o' them a. Traditional Scots song[1]

Private J C Forbes, The Menin Gate Memorial, Ypres

On 28 July 1914, James Forbes and Louis Middleton were the future: James was the youngest of the Forbes family, the nineteen-year-old wee brother among five fledging Forbes farmers; and Louis, the first-born son, the eighteen-year-old medical student and doctor-in-waiting for his father's Peterhead practice. A year later great Uncle James was no more and, by the end of the war, Uncle Louis was severely and irretrievably psychologically damaged.

Private James C Forbes *2nd Lt Louis W J Middleton*

IN FLANDERS SOD[2]

Wi' beardless lads scarce by wi' school
But eager as the lave to list. Charles Murray[3]

At the start of war, these two braves were students at Aberdeen University, the cream of the crop from the rural North East. They were strapping lads raised on country fare and ample fish (unlike city boys. Half the volunteers from jute city Dundee were turned down as insufficiently fit for enlisting). By the end of the war they were the past, their demise casting a century-long shadow over their families, my family: The two grieving clans, Middleton and Forbes, were later united, during the next war, by the marriage of my parents, Mary Isobel Forbes and John Middleton. My wartime legacy? An inheritance of sorrow.

100

War Memorial, Fordyce Academy, Banffshire

My mother's uncle, James Clapperton Forbes, was born on 23 February 1895. There had been seven siblings, but two died of tuberculosis. My great Uncle James was born at Cowhythe, a farm near Portsoy, amongst the gently undulating Banffshire barley fields and farmland that dips down to the Moray Firth. His parents were William Forbes MBE and Agnes Jane McRobie. My mother didn't say much about her grandfather other than a wry 'he was a local councillor'. The canny paterfamilias decreed that all his boys should work in the North of Scotland Bank (later amalgamated with the Clydesdale Bank, which at the time of writing has recently merged with Virgin Money). This was preparatory to a life in farming. I don't recall my mother ever speaking about her grandmother.

Fordyce Academy was in the traditional Scottish style of all-round public education, public in the sense of non-fee-paying and open to all. From there James Forbes was admitted to Aberdeen University where he studied agriculture from 1911-14.

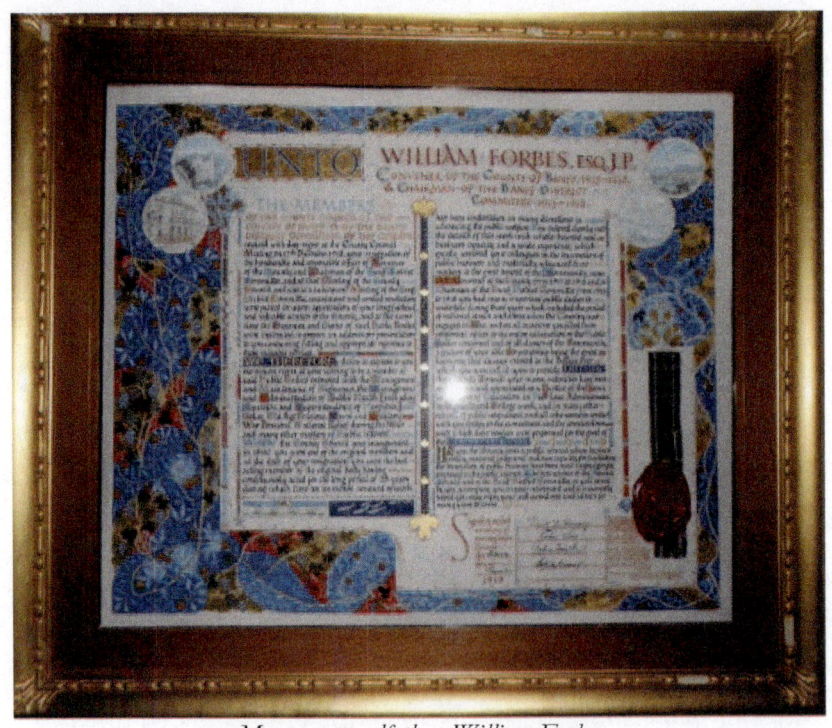

My great-grandfather, William Forbes

Whilst at college, the young farmer joined the Officer Training Corps (OTC), which offered camaraderie and, in the days before farmers having holidays and foreign recreational travel, a desirable two-week summer camping in the Black Isle. When these *loons* ('boys' in Doric), mostly teenagers, joined the Territorials, they made themselves available for home service only. It would have been inconceivable to them that this would entail fighting an actual foreign war. When war threatened in 1914, however, most of them were carried along by the fervour and agreed to serve overseas.

When war was declared James Forbes was at summer camp in Tain, on the northern side of the Moray Firth. The student soldiers were recalled to Aberdeen and by the autumn of 1914 they had been ordered south to train for war.

The 4th Gordon Highlanders returning to Aberdeen from Tain, 1915.

The Aberdeen University OTC formed the U Company of the 4th Battalion Gordon Highlanders, a celebrated unit of student soldiers. They were the sole company of student soldiers in the entire British Expeditionary Force. U Company, however, was later controversially renamed the D Company, after amalgamation with the Aberdeen Grammar School (my late father's school) and Robert Gordon's College D Company. (My Uncle Louis Middleton was in the 5th Gordons, the Buchan Brigade.)

> *I've listed! Dang the nowt an' neeps!*
> *I'm aff to fecht or fa'.* Mary Symon[4]

James went with the student battalion to the douce environs of the south of England to train for war. 18,000 *sojers* from the Highland Regiments descended upon the unsuspecting residents of Bedford. This episode was a novel experience for both pawky Scotsmen and local southerners alike. These educated Caledonians needed little encouragement to play up to the image of the kilted barbarian.[5]

> U Company... *found temporary billets in the suburb of 'Oney'ill', and our first week there almost convinced the artisan residents that we were semi-savages.*

> *They stood in their doorways and gaped at us when we danced an eightsome reel in the street.*[6]
>
> *Then, in addition to our 12,000 infantry, we had no fewer than twelve pipe bands... Our invasion was a peaceful penetration – from the military point of view – but we shattered the calm of 700 years.*[7]

There was ample opportunity for linguistic caper:

> *English Colonel to Highland sentry: 'Who are you?'*
> *Sentry to the Colonel: 'Fine Sir, and hoo's yersel?'*[8]

The cocky 4th Gordons of U Company were a novelty to the Cockney sergeant majors. The southerners in peaked caps were more used to dealing with compliant young Englishmen. The U Company – Aberdeen University undergraduates and recent graduates, young men used to debating issues – were generally willing to obey orders, sensible ones, but were unlikely to comply with the apparently ridiculous. They took a dim view, for example, of the requirement to lay spare laces in the exact same place every day during kit inspection.[9]

In his *History of the Fifty First (Highland) Division 1914–1918*, Major F W Bewsher writes of the Division in the early days of the war:

> *The 'barrack' discipline was excellent, but the field discipline left much to be desired. It was sometime before some COs even could be made to understand that an order in the field did not admit of heated argument before execution; and the rank and file had to learn that training was not a recreation to stop when they got tired.*[10]

There would have been ample opportunity for *sotto voce* mutterings of *Awa 'n' bile yer heed in tattie broth*, or similar.

Other regimental sergeant majors were less tolerant. The rough justice intensified in the heat of battle and when these young men were at their most weary, 'insubordination' could be penalised by field punishments such as 'crucifixion' – being tied to the wheels of a wagon in the shape of an X, as described by Robert Graves[11]. This punishment was meted out to Graves' loyal servant, Private Fahy, by the fierce-looking battalion police sergeant for drunkenness in the field, after meeting up with an old friend from years back in India.

Graves relates another occasion when the punishment was inflicted on an NCO for the heinous crime of addressing a corporal by his Christian name, calling him 'his petit-caporal *Jacquot*'.[12]

But back in Bedford the 'cocky wee Gordons' eventually knuckled down and 'all this gradually wore off, and in less than three months, units began to assume a workmanlike and even serviceable appearance on parade.'[13]

James was mobilised in August 1914 and the 4th Gordons crossed the Channel in February 1915 for what was described as the 'great adventure'.

There was the commonly held belief amongst the combatants that the war would be 'over by Christmas'. The generals, however, knew otherwise, according to historian Hew Strachan in a lecture on 14 October 2014.[14] 'Truth is the first casualty of war' is an old adage attributed a century ago to US Republican Senator Hiram Warren Johnson, one-time Governor of California.

THE PARTING GLASS

(TRADITIONAL SCOTS SONG)

O' all the money that e'er I spent
I spent it in good company,
And all the harm that e'er I've done
Alas, it was to none but me.
And all I've done for want of wit
To memory now I can't recall,
So fill to me the parting glass
Good night and joy be with you all.

My mother related the family tale that when Uncle James came to say goodbye her eyes were fixated on her young uncle. The parting Gordon Highlander asked my grandparents to 'turn that bairn's face away'. My mother, being only fifteen months at the time, was too young to remember this, but the parting – or the family tale about James' departure – was firmly etched in her mind forever. Years later she surmised that she had been transfixed by his shiny buttons. Or maybe there was an unspoken sense that he might never see 'that bairn' again. He didn't.

To summarise:

- Aberdeen University U Company of the 4th Battalion Gordon Highlanders was the only company of student soldiers to serve in the British Expeditionary Force.
- They crossed the Channel in February 1915.
- By September 1915 half these young men had fallen on the battlefields of Flanders and the University Unit ceased to exist.

The fresh-faced Gordon Highlander, Private James C Forbes

A sojer, head to heel, Banffshire poet, Mary Symon [15]

U Company left for France on the evening of 19 February 1915 on the *Archimedes*, a filthy old cattle boat. They were 'packed like sardines'.[16] Uncle James reached Le Havre the following morning. In true Scots style they were piped to Bleville Camp. To the delight of the French, *les Écossais* sang *La Marseillaise*. The young Scotsmen were less than thrilled however with the beer that awaited them in the *estaminets*, the café-bars in northern France and Belgium.

En route to La Clytte they saw their first batch of men coming back from the firing line. Alexander Rule, a diarist in U Company, observes 'some ghastly and at last gasp'.[17] They then sewed buttonholes for braces into their kilts 'to prevent their unwanted descent'.[18] With the men's loss of weight in the trenches and the weight of mud on their clothing, gravity could pull inconveniently at kilts.

'Saw shell bursting for the 1st time!' further comments Rule.[19] The 4th Gordons were girding their loins, shortly to be in the trenches. They arrived at La Clytte, near the ancient Belgian city of Ypres ('Wipers' in Tommy-speak). By the end of the war, this striking medieval city had been flattened. (It was faithfully rebuilt after the war.)

By 27 February these young Gordons were in trenches at La Clytte, which is five miles from Ypres. From then until mid-May they were engaged in moving between the trenches and their rest area at nearby Locre.[20] The Gordons' introduction to 'Flanders sod' was in improving trenches while under the threat of sniping and artillery.

In no time at all they were in the thick of it. Fellow A Company went into the trenches on 1 March. Alexander Rule continues 'So this is the real thing at last.[21] On 7 March 1915, when U Company were on parade, they heard death sentences read out for desertion – and they were carried out. *Pour encourager les autres.*[22]

On 17 March 1915, the first member of this U Company of varsity pals died in battle. He was called Lance Corporal William Scott. This was the beginning of the slaughter of these innocents. During the earlier part of the conflict the dead were taken back from the trenches and given a Christian burial. As the fighting intensified they were buried where they lay, if it were possible, and if they were found at all.

ALL THE SAD HORSES

We didn't know much about it.
We'd thought they'd all come back
But off they all were taken
White and brown and black;
Cart and cab and carriage,
Wagon and break and dray,
Went out at the call of duty
And we watched them go away.
All of the grieving owners
Let them along the lane
Down the hill to the station,
And saw them off by train. [23]

The Kelpies: steel installations honouring the Clydesdale, the workhorse of Scotland

Alexander Rule's diary entry from Vierstraat on 22 March notes 'Few bodies (men, horses, cows etc behind) - utterly out of place in a sunbathed landscape'.[24] The slain horses would have held a particular resonance for these Aberdeenshire and Banffshire *loons* (lads). Many, like James Forbes, came from farms with a number of Clydesdale horses, their trusty steeds in the days before *tractors hae replaced ma horse*.[25]

Scotland's native heavy horse, the Clydesdale, was called upon to serve the country during the First World War, but at what cost? Quarter of a million horses belonging to the British were lost at the Western Front. Sixty thousand were lost to enemy fire.[26] Eight million horses, donkeys and mules died in the First World War.[27] Just as the soldiers were cut down by guns, shells, gas, disease and appalling conditions, so were the horses. As with human beings, what could protect a horse from gunfire and shelling, and the sheer terror of their predicament? As Mary Bromilow, author of *The Clydesdale: Workhorse of the World*[28] outlined, it was accepted that wars were the creation of human beings, but animals had not chosen the dreadful fate that was inflicted upon them. Most of the horses perished, in fact, as a result of the unspeakable conditions. Although strong and sturdy, the Clydesdale is a vulnerable *cratur* (creature), susceptible to pneumonia and to foot infections on account of their iconic 'feathers', the glorious white hair that flows over their hooves.

IN THE THICK OF IT *ENCORE*

As the D Company's deployment advanced, Field Punishment Number One, 'crucifixation', was carried out on their wee pal Gamin Anderson for sleeping in the trenches on 17–21 April 1915. The laddie from Portknockie was nicknamed 'Gammon' after the smoke from his briar pipe and refined to 'Gamin', meaning 'urchin', on account of his diminutive stature. Gamin had been at Fordyce Academy, like Uncle James, and had then studied Arts at Aberdeen University. The unfortunate Gamin was strapped to a wheel with his arms outstretched and his legs tied together for up to two hours a day.[29]

This could on occasion be carried out within range of enemy fire. Gamin had been tired after looking after a wounded colleague, Corporal Hawes.[30] The powers that be had failed to mention that pertinent fact to their commanding officer in extenuation.

Aberdeenshire lad Alexander Rule, adds to his diary insert of 17-21 April his observations about local agriculture: there was a '*nettoyage* system hive of activity in smallish plots. Cultv (sic) by bullock or one-horse plough – work from early morn till late.'[31]

On 29 April 1915, Private James Forbes wrote to his brother Alex:

> *…The cocoa and milk is the very thing we want when in the trenches as it is very easily made and far more sustaining than tea. It was very good of you to get it sent to me so soon.*[32]

By mid-May 1915, nineteen of James' platoon pals were slain, but he says nothing of this in his letters home.

Gas canisters seen at Hooge in 2014

The Germans introduced chlorine gas at Ypres on 22 April 1915. This was a war crime. It was contrary to the 1899 Hague Declaration concerning Asphyxiating Gases and the 1907 Hague Convention on Land Warfare forbidding the use of 'poison or poisoned weapons' in warfare.

The British were driven back by a gas attack on 23 April at Kemmel. On the same day, these young men keenly felt the loss of D company singer, Sandy Skinner. 'No more "Maid of Morven" in Sandy's tenor voice' [33]:

Have you seen the rose in bloom
Blushing on its thorny bough?
Have ye seen the modest primrose
Bending 'neath the silver dew?

Soon, too soon, the restless ocean
Shall bear me far, far away,
But the love I bear my chosen
Ne'er can from this poor heart stray?

Deeply hid like miser's treasure,
Lives thine image in its core;
But ah me! sweet Maid of Morven,
I must leave thee evermore.[34]

The 4th Gordons were at Rozenhill at Hill 60 on 10 May 1915 and from there they saw Ypres ablaze on May 12. They moved to Zillebecke, two miles south east of Ypres, where new trenches were dug. On 16 May, the Gordons were practising gas defences, which were to prove pitifully inadequate to the task.[35] D company moved the same day to Zillebecke. On 25 May 1915 they moved west along the Menin Road to Hooge. On 2 June there was a German attack, which was driven off.

NEEPS AND TATTIES

Ever the Forbes farmer, James wrote to his brother Alex on 7 June 1915:

I expect you will have all the turnips down now… We have not been under a roof for a fortnight… I envy you and Charlie [36] very much being able to bathe… I found a potato field near a ruined farm here so we have been living on 'spuds'… Our staple diet when in the trenches was bully beef and biscuits…It does not do to think of the food I got at home as that makes you 'fed up' or in plain fact a little homesick.[37]

Y Wood (highlighted in green) on the Menin Road, Hooge, just outside Ypres

There was shelling onto the battalion on 15 June and a retaliatory attack was planned. The wire was cut in preparation for an assault on the Germans, which was postponed to 16 June. The attack on Y Wood was successful, but followed by the inevitable German counterattack. The battalion withdrew through the night of 16–17 June 1915.

'10 men were recorded as killed, including I assume Private Forbes.' [38] According to this Gordon Highlanders Museum report, the body of twenty-one-year-old Private James Clapperton Forbes, was never found, but see below.

Conflicting accounts of the events around 16 June resound with chaos, confusion, and compassion. On an exploratory tour of this area in Belgium in 2014, I discovered that gas had entered the German arsenal around that time, but none of this was recorded in the accounts that I had found specifically about my great uncle James' death - neither regimental nor familial - before then. James' friend, Marshall Ledingham, son of the local schoolmaster at Boyndie School (where my mother was later to go) penned a gentle epistle to James' mother (my great-grandmother) on 25 June 1915. I think this was an attempt to spare her the reality, as his body was never found. (Those not found were remembered on the Menin Gate, as James was.) Reading this letter, or telling this tale, never fails to disassemble me:

> ... *James was sleeping in a traverse along with four others. In this place we had placed all our machine guns and equipment. Whether the place had been spotted by an aeroplane or not we do not know but the shells came over quickly and the third one landed in the traverse. James was killed instantly and another varsity man Sergeant Duncan was very badly wounded.*
> *In the evening we buried him in a little garden where many of our battalion are. James' death was very keenly felt by the whole section and by me in particular. Ever since we left Bedford we have been together. Many a time did we speak of bathing at Dallachy, and the morning of his death he remarked to me that you and Mrs Forbes of Dallachy* [39] *had been down for a dip.* [40]

D Company was relieved at midnight, but it is reported on the battalion website that seven men were killed and one was missing. On further searching the 4th Gordons website I found the words and the confirmation I had dreaded, that there was German gas as well as shrapnel shelling on 16 June.[41] Again, I refer to the war poets to communicate the unbearable.

DULCE ET DECORUMA EST Wilfred Owen[42]

Bent double, like old beggars under sacks,
Knock-kneed, coughing like hags, we cursed through sludge,
Till on the haunting flares we turned our backs,
And towards our distant rest began to trudge.
Men marched asleep. Many had lost their boots,
But limped on, blood-shod. All went lame; all blind;
Drunk with fatigue; deaf even to the hoots
Of gas-shells dropping softly behind.

Gas! GAS! Quick, boys!—An ecstasy of fumbling
Fitting the clumsy helmets just in time,
But someone still was yelling out and stumbling
And flound'ring like a man in fire or lime.
Dim through the misty panes and thick green light,
He plunges at me, guttering, choking, drowning.
In all my dreams before my helpless sight,
He plunges at me, guttering choking, drowning.
in some smothering dreams, you too could pace
Behind the wagon that we flung him in,
And watch the white eyes writhing in his face,
His hanging face, like a devil's sick of sin;
If you could hear, at every jolt, the blood
Come gargling from the froth-corrupted lungs,
Obscene as cancer, bitter as the cud
Of vile, incurable sores on innocent tongues,—
My friend, you would not tell with such high zest
To children ardent for some desperate glory,
The old Lie: Dulce et decorum est
Pro patria mori.

War Memorial, Fordyce

I experienced a whiff of chlorine gas myself and the ensuing panic in a chemistry class at school. To differentiate gases, one of the properties we were taught to explore was smell. We were required to put our nose into the bell jars and to sniff the gas. On this particular occasion I had a cold and smelt nothing. Like many in our school, the chemistry teacher had had a Second World War history, and according to my brother, had been with bomber command. His words are indelibly marked on my brain: 'Put your hooter right in it and take a good deep breath', which I dutifully did. I could not breathe. I coughed and spluttered and was unable to communicate my distress. I think he thought I was play acting. Ultimately he realised I was in genuine distress and was struggling for breath. I was eventually sent home to my doctor mother.

A century later, the horrors of gas warfare were being reported from Syria. This twenty-first century horror was allegedly orchestrated by Bashar Al-Assad, former ophthalmologist at the then Western Ophthalmic (now Eye) Hospital, past of St Mary's Hospital, my first place of work in London.[43] By way of balance in this tale, the consultant neurologist when I was there was Roger Bannister, who had been a sports hero. He had broken the four-minute mile record in the fifties.[44] Coincidently Roger Bannister was awarded another degree at the Sheldonian Theatre in Oxford when my husband was being awarded his Advanced Diploma in Local History in 2010. To remind, cousin Louis Thomson, the only survivor of these First World War remembrances, had previously studied medicine at St Mary's Hospital.

Gas was introduced at the Second Battle of Ypres, which appears to have been the cause of death of this fledgling farmer, James Forbes. It was developed by German Jewish Fritz Haber.[45] He was thought to be the father of chemical warfare in developing chorine and phosgene gas. By way of contrast, Haber would later transform the Forbes farmers' fields, as well as agriculture the world over, with his Nobel Prize winning nitrogen fertiliser. In 1909 he had found a way to synthesise ammonia from nitrogen and hydrogen, and it went on to be manufactured on a massive scale. He continued after the First World War to develop further poison gases including Zyklon B, a cyanide-based gas. This gas would later be used by the Nazis to terrible effect in their death camps. Even some of Haber's Jewish relatives were victims.

If gas wasn't bad enough, young James was spared another terror yet to come, the truly horrifying *Flammenwerfer*, the portable flamethrower. The *Flammenwerfer* was later used to terrifying effect at Hooge on 30 July 1915.

Great Uncle James' name is engraved on Panel 38 of the Menin Gate Memorial at Ypres. His sacrifice is also listed at the mighty Scottish War Memorial at Edinburgh Castle, in the Gordon Highlanders' war memorial book. The regimental entries are of those Scots who had laid down their lives for their country. I would suggest a visit to the Scottish War Memorial at Edinburgh Castle be a requisite experience for all schoolchildren in Scotland to introduce them to the monumental folly that was in my view the First World War.

He is also named all over the North East of Scotland, including the University of Aberdeen Roll of Honour,[46] Fordyce Academy, Fordyce cemetery, the Portsoy War Memorial and nearby Whitehills. These war memorials in these little dear Scottish villages shock with the quantity of local men lost in the two world wars. The proliferation of these granite memorials is huge.

Was it only yesterday
Lusty comrades marched away?
Now they're covered up with clay.
Patrick MacGill [47]

Portsoy War Memorial

A TALE OF TWO YS

The author at Y Wood, Hooge, near Ypres, Belgium, 2014

I believe if the dead come back at all they'll come back green
to grow from the broken earth and drink the gathered water
and all the things they suffered will mean no more to them
than the setting-in of the ordinary dark, or a change of weather.
John Glenday[48]

It is hard for me to articulate my feelings about the tragedy of young great Uncle James' slaughter. I look again to the poets, such as John Glenday, to grasp the grief and render it communicable. Also from Broughty Ferry, poet John Glenday had had two shell shocked uncles in the First World War. He was the first person I knowingly met with a similar war family scenario. I was very pleased to meet him at a study day on poetry about the First World War and to share experiences with him.

James Forbes was lost at Y Wood in Flanders, echoing fellow Gordon Highlander and Aberdeen University student, Louis Middleton, at Y Ravine in France: two young men united by *alma mater*, sacrifice, and posthumously hope, when in the next war James Forbes' niece, my mother, Mary Isobel Forbes, married Louis Middleton's younger brother, my father, John Middleton. Destroyed, presumably by shellfire, Y Wood is no longer woodland, but a pastoral scene of pastureland in the heart of rural Belgium; whilst, in France, at Beaumont-Hamel's Y Ravine, sheep gently graze.

Trench near Y Ravine Cemetery, Beaumont Hamel, France

AFTERMATH

My grandfather, Charlie Forbes, and his brothers, suffered throughout their lives with the loss of their wee brother. Grandpa Forbes had wanted to travel down through Britain and across the Channel to search for his missing brother in 1915 but, as far as I know, this never happened. My grandfather never recovered from the loss of young James, nor indeed did his brother, Alex. Both suffered from profound depression for the rest of their days.

A century after the death of James Forbes, I represented the family on a pilgrimage to Y Wood in Belgium, where the young farmer had been fatally struck down. As far as I know, no other family member had made this painful journey. This was the day after my gruelling visit to France's Y Valley, the place of Uncle Louis Middleton's last stand. It was especially poignant that a familiar horse was pastured in this now gentle Belgian farmland at Y Wood, and trotted gently towards me. There were there no trees, nor graves, nor memorials that I could see to indicate the horror that once convulsed this flat, unremarkable, rural part of the world. I left my own little cross for this lost member of the Catholic branch of the family.

Farm horse, Y Wood

Private James Clapperton Forbes is remembered on the Menin Gate. This huge monument is a vivid testimonial to man's inhumanity to man. It is to pay tribute to those lost in the Great War and whose remains had not been found. That Uncle James is honoured there would seem to contradict the sentiments expressed in the letter written to my great grandmother by James' friend, Marshall Ledingham. He wrote that James had been buried in the battlefield along with the other lost members of their battalion. It seems to me that James' friend, Marshall, may have been trying to spare my great grandmother horror. I have no knowledge, however, of how thorough the search would have been after battle to retrieve the remains of these lost young men. That my grandfather, James' older brother, Charlie, wanted to travel to Flanders to search for his wee brother, seems to support the view that James' remains were never found.

THE KINDERMORD

The final throws of the Second Battle of Ypres have been thought to be a bitter German revenge for the deaths of the *Kindermord,* their own student soldiers, slain in autumn 1914 at the Battle of Langemark, at the First Battle of Ypres. German dead are buried in the shady Langemark Cemetery.

Langemark Cemetry

The Germans claimed that seventy-five per cent of their soldiers were student volunteers who went into battle singing *Deutschland uber alles*. The German tale of the 'massacre of the innocents' was, however, later found to be shrouded in exaggeration and myth. The actual number of German student soldiers was less than half that number, and the stories of soldiers singing into battle questionable. This, it would seem, was a smokescreen to disguise the dismal performance of more experienced combatants, in spite of the Germans outnumbering the opposition. An alternative reading could have been that it was a ruse to divert attention from the use of gas, illegal in international law.[49]

The alleged loss of so many young German students was later exploited to great effect by one Adolf Hitler at Langemark cemetery on 1 June 1940, and also in *Mein Kampf*. Hitler had served with the 16th Reserved Bavarian Regiment in Belgium, as well as France, during the First World War. He had fought south of Ypres in the area of Wytschaete on the Messines Ridge. He was apparently temporarily blinded by a British Gas attack near Ypres in 1918.

The mythology surrounding *Der Kindermord bei Ypern* accrued powerful valency for the Third Reich. Actual traumatic events live long too in popular memory. Centuries after the Serbs were defeated by the Turks on 15 June 1389 at Kosovo, this event is still ingrained in Serb memory and can be tapped. Nearer to home, the decimation of the Jacobites at Culloden on 16 April 1746 lives on in many a Scots soul. The latter two seismic events had some bearing upon the fate of the third protagonist in our tale, cousin Dr Louis Thomson, to be explored in the next chapter.

Deep psychic wounds in national identity, especially after an injustice has been perceived to have been perpetrated on a population, can be accessed in a call to arms. Folk memories, such as these – apocryphal or actual - live on powerfully in national cultures, and can be employed to great political advantage. Hitler understood all too well the potential when visiting Langemark on the first of June, 1940.

Hitler at Langemark Cemetery, 1 June 1940

Langemark on my visit in 2014

REFERENCES

[1] Traditional Scots song
[2] Symon, M, (1938) A recruit for the Gordons IN Deveron days. Aberdeen: D Wyllie & Son.
[3] Symon, M, (1938) A recruit for the Gordons IN Deveron days. Aberdeen: D Wyllie & Son.
[4] Symon, M (1938) A recruit for the Gordons. IN Deveron days. Aberdeen: D. Wylie & Son.
[5] Rule A (1934) Students Under Arms, Aberdeen: Aberdeen University Press.
[6] Rule A (1934) Students Under Arms, Aberdeen: Aberdeen University Press.
[7] Rule A (1934) Students Under Arms, Aberdeen: Aberdeen University Press.
[8] Rule A (1934) Students Under Arms, Aberdeen: Aberdeen University Press.
[9] Rule A (1934) Students Under Arms, Aberdeen: Aberdeen University Press.
[10] Bewsher, FW (1921) The history of the 51st (Highland) Division Edinburgh and London: William Blackwood and Sons.
[11] Graves, R (1929) Goodbye to all that. London: Jonathan Cape 1929.
[12] Graves, R (1929) Goodbye to all that. London: Jonathan Cape 1929.
[13] Bewsher, FW (1921) The history of the 51st (Highland) Division Edinburgh and London: William Blackwood and Sons.
[14] Strachan, H. Haldane, Haig and Hamilton: The mobilisation of Scotland in 1914. The Caledonian lecture 14 October 2014.
[15] Symon, M (1938) A recruit for the Gordons IN Deveron days. Aberdeen: D. Wyllie & Son.
[16] Shanks, GJ (2015) Yet another glorious day. The 1915 World War 1 Diary of Alexander Rule Stonehaven: Graham J Shanks.
[17] Shanks, GJ (2015) Yet another glorious day. The 1915 World War 1 Diary of Alexander Rule Stonehaven: Graham J Shanks.
[18] Shanks, GJ (2015) Yet another glorious day. The 1915 World War 1 Diary of Alexander Rule Stonehaven: Graham J Shanks.
[19] Shanks, GJ (2015) Yet another glorious day. The 1915 World War 1 Diary of Alexander Rule Stonehaven: Graham J Shanks.
[20] Private email from the Gordon Highlander museum 2 September 2014.
[21] Shanks, GJ (2015) Yet another glorious day. The 1915 World War 1 Diary of Alexander Rule Stonehaven: Graham J Shanks.
[22] Shanks, GJ (2015) Yet another glorious day. The 1915 World War 1 Diary of Alexander Rule Stonehaven: Graham J Shanks.
[23] Royal Society for Prevention of Cruelty to Animals (RSPCA) 1916 Allegory in aid of funds for wounded horses

[24] Shanks, GJ (2015) Yet another glorious day. The 1915 World War 1 Diary of Alexander Rule Stonehaven: Graham J Shanks.
[25] Steele, D The last trip home.
[26] Bromilow, M (2011) The Clydesdale: workhorse of the world. 2011. Glendaruel: Argyll Publishing.
[27] http://www.animalsinwar.org.uk/index.cfm?asset_id=1375. Searched 14 March 2018.
[28] Bromilow, M (2011) The Clydesdale: workhorse of the world. 2011. Glendaruel: Argyll Publishing.
[29] Shanks, GJ (2015) Yet another glorious day. The 1915 World War 1 Diary of Alexander Rule Stonehaven: Graham J Shanks.
[30] Shanks, GJ (2015) Yet another glorious day. The 1915 World War 1 Diary of Alexander Rule Stonehaven: Graham J Shanks.
[31] Shanks, GJ (2015) Yet another glorious day. The 1915 World War 1 Diary of Alexander Rule Stonehaven: Graham J Shanks.
[32] Letter from James Forbes to Alex Forbes 29 April 2015
[33] Shanks, GJ (2015) Yet another glorious day. The 1915 World War 1 Diary of Alexander Rule Stonehaven: Graham J Shanks.
[34] Maid of Morven. Traditional Scots song
[35] Shanks, GJ (2015) Yet another glorious day. The 1915 World War 1 Diary of Alexander Rule Stonehaven: Graham J Shanks.
[36] Charles Forbes, author's grandfather.
[37] Letter from James Forbes to Alex Forbes
[38] Private communication, 2 September 2014 Gordon Highlanders Museum. (I do not have any knowledge of the little garden referred to.)
[39] Mary Forbes, author's grandmother
[40] Letter from Marshall Ledingham to my great-grandmother, Mrs Forbes.
[41] www.4thgordons.com searched 31 March 2017 and 2 May 2018.
[42] Owen W, 1920 Dulce et decorum est. IN Poems London: Chatto & Windus.
[43] https://www.armscontrol.org/factsheets/Timeline-of-Syrian-Chemical-Weapons-Activity Searched. 10 September 2021
[44] https://medstars.co.uk/blog/waiting-room/1135/. Searched 10 September 2021
[45] McKie, R (3 Nov 2013) 'From fertiliser to Zyklon B: 100 years of the scientific discovery that brought life and death.' The Observer.
[46] Aberdeen University Roll of Service, 1921. ed. Desborough Allardyce, M., published 1921.
[47] MacGill P (1917) After Loos (Café Pierre le Blanc, Nouex les Mines, Michaelmas Even, 1915 IN Soldier Songs. London: Jenkins.
[48] Glenday J. The big push. http://poetrysociety.org.uk/poems/the-big-push. Searched 18 July 2018
[49] http://mentalfloss.com/article/59593/wwi-centennial-apocalypse-ypres. Searched 23 January 2017 & 2 May 2018

CHAPTER 7

ANOTHER LOST BOY?

If something is going to happen to me, I want to be there. Albert Camus[1]

Dr Louis Thomson with one of his Cairn terriers

Breathes there the man, with soul so dead,
Who never to himself hath said,
This is my own, my native land!
Whose heart hath ne'er within him burn'd,
As home his footsteps he hath turn'd
From wandering on a foreign strand!
If such there breathe, go, mark him well;
For him no Minstrel raptures swell;
High though his titles, proud his name,
Boundless his wealth as wish can claim;
Despite those titles, power, and pelf,
The wretch, concentred all in self,
Living, shall forfeit fair renown,
And, doubly dying, shall go down
To the vile dust, from whence he sprung,
Unwept, unhonour'd, and unsung.[2]

Au contraire! The émigré Dr Louis Léopold Arthur William Thomson emerged from World War One laden with honours from both the Serbian and the French governments – though estranged for some time from his ostensible parents and his native land.

> **SERBIAN HONOUR TO SCOTSMAN**
>
> Well-merited distinctions have been conferred on Dr William Arthur Leopold Louis Thomson and Mrs Thomson, Etrochey, France, for the services they rendered during the second Serbian retreat. On Dr Thomson has been bestowed the Order of the White Eagle and on Mrs Thomson the Order of St Sava by his Highness the Prince Regent of Serbia as a public mark of homage for the services done to the Serbian people during the year 1915. Dr Thomson is an M.D. of Lyons, and also holds the degrees of M.R.C.S. and L.R.C.P. He is a Scotsman by birth, and a cousin of Mrs Dr Middleton, Queen Street, Peterhead, and a nephew of Mrs Heslop, Howe o' Buchan.

The Aberdeen Daily Journal, Tuesday 23 October 1917

The Prince Regent of Serbia awarded Louis the *Order of the White Eagle*, while the *Order of Saint Sava* was bestowed upon his courageous companion, his Nantaise wife Jean Marie Bordelais. These were public marks of honour for the couple's unstinting devotion to the Serbian people. After serving throughout the devastating typhus epidemic of 1915, the doctor and his wife then accompanied the Serbian army over the high mountains to Albania during the harrowing Great Retreat. Louis was later honoured by the French government with the *Croix de Guerre* and the *Legion d'honneur*.

SHADES OF THE WHITE COCKADE?

Charles Edward Stuart

So who was this third, more distantly related uncle in my extended family – an apparent descendant of a hunted Jacobite? Did this romantic European background sew imaginative seeds in the young Louis' mind? Did this family history inspire the young Scots doctor to live and work in France and to serve in Serbia in 1915 – as a Frenchman?

As with the first two brave hearts, I never met this hero, but an air of intrigue surrounded him – and still does. But there was one fundamental difference between Louis Thomson and my other two World War One uncles: Louis Thomson not only survived the war but, along with his wife, continued to enjoy a long, interesting and fruitful life. No post-war resting on his laurels, though, or forever harking back to 'the war'. He was in fact set to make a mark in France throughout the rest of his life – but not in the Caledonian land of his seeming origins.

Curiously, this supremely well-connected young man had emigrated from the royal realm at Kensington Palace (where his apparent father, Uncle Willie, was page to Princess Louise, Queen Victoria's artistic daughter) to a secluded corner of rural France, his adopted matrilineal land, where he embraced the life of a country doctor in Burgundy. But having acquired a taste for adventure during the war in Serbia – and survived – this swash-buckling adventurer continued his engagement with the international scene later in life, as well as contributing to his local community as a social reformer.

Louis Thomson was the only one of the three family men in this tale to escape the mud of the Western Front. He was, however, to suffer other unimaginable war-time horrors elsewhere – in southeastern Europe, in Serbia. He documented this gruelling episode in his book *La Retraite de Serbie: Octobre–Décembre 1915*.[3] In that beleaguered country he tended to typhus sufferers, then joined the Serb people and their army in their tragic retreat to the Adriatic in an heroic effort to escape massacre by the Germans, Austro-Hungarians and Bulgarians. The ghastly aspects of the typhus epidemic and the other war-time horrors endured are curiously understated in Louis' book.

THE BALKAN BLACK DEATH

The crowlin ferlie Robert Burns[4]

So how did this young doctor brought up by a Scotsman and a Frenchwoman in London, come to live and work in France, and to serve as a doctor in Serbia in 1915? The besieged Balkan country had suffered a terrible typhus epidemic early on in the First World War and had put out a call for international medical assistance.[5] Typhus had been endemic in Serbia, and the local people had some immunity, but the *rickettsia prowazekii*, the typhus-bearing bacterium, was to prove fatal to northern Europeans with no immunity. The exposure of

Austrian prisoners-of-war and their dispersal throughout Serbia was thought to have drastically spread the disease.

The bacteria were carried by body lice, which were rampant in soldiers' clothes in the dire conditions of war. Typhus never took hold in the deplorable conditions of the trenches of the Western Front, despite the torment caused to combatants by the *crowlin ferlie*, the louse, immortalised by Robert Burns.[6] Men in the trenches would while away the hours between action catching and incinerating the wretched beasties. Tormented by the itching, the soldiers would scratch, so expelling louse excreta into the skin and causing infection. The lice spread Trench Fever on the Western Front, a severely debilitating disease to which 520,000 British troops succumbed. One victim, the writer J R R Tolkien, was invalided out because of it, and wrote *The Hobbit*[7] and *The Lord of the Rings*[8] when recovering. His vivid descriptions were informed by his experiences at the Somme:

> *They lie in all the pools, pale faces, deep deep under the dark water. I saw them: grim faces and evil, and noble faces and sad. Many faces proud and fair, and weeds in their silver hair. But all foul, all rotting, all dead.*[9]

But typhus was a disease of a different order altogether. By the end of 1914 one in six Serbs had succumbed to this medieval blight and over 200,000 had died from the disease. The country boasted only four hundred doctors, having lost doctors and nurses to warfare or disease in the recent Balkan Wars, and with no time to train and regain medical staff.[10] Louis Thomson was by this time a senior doctor in the French army and responded to the Serbian appeal for medical aid.[11] The young doctor and his wife set off for Serbia to help with the epidemic in the spring of 1915; they then accompanied the Serbs in their arduous retreat over the mountains to the sea.[12]

AN ENIGMA

But why had Louis Thomson left this island before the war to become a doctor in the small Burgundy town of Châtillon-sur-Seine? Why was he awarded the Order of the White Eagle by the Prince Regent of

Serbia? And why did the French government bestow upon him the *Croix de Guerre* and the *Legion d'honneur*?

The young doctor

Who was this dashing Franco-Scot with the liquid eyes? Whether a Saxe-Coburg or a Highlander by birth, his ostensible adoptive parents were the Thomsons of Crathie post office, and the family were the direct descendants of hunted Jacobites from Speyside. Charles Thomson was the first postmaster at Crathie: he had been a keeper at Balmoral when it was owned by Sir Robert Gordon, and was appointed postmaster in 1843. When Prince Albert, Queen Victoria's consort, bought Balmoral in 1852, Charles Thomson was retained as forester and postmaster.

Charles Thomson, first postmaster at Crathie

As outlined earlier, our family believe (and have circumstantial evidence) that Louis Thomson was the illegitimate son of Princess Louise. My nursing-sister auntie knew the impossibility of the gestation dates of a baby in relation to Marie and William Thomson. Childless Uncle Willie and Aunt Marie had accompanied Princess Louise in her posting to Canada, and came back with baby Louis. The dates did not fit.

GOODBYE TO ALL THAT

Louis' parents? William and Marie Thomson

Before the war Louis had lived in London. As the winds of war were gathering, he left abruptly for France, never to live in the UK again, although he always retained his British citizenship. Like another Francophile Scot, Robert Louis Stevenson, he changed his name: he dropped the patronymic 'William', the name of his adoptive father. Louis' grandson, Toulouse resident Jean-Max Thomson, thinks Louis was bored with the United Kingdom; and he didn't like the British difficulty with his name, a country more familiar with the feminine Louise, than the masculine Louis.

 I can certainly understand the appeal of France, the French climate no doubt proving more appealing than the foggy London town of those days, and certainly warmer than Aberdeeenshire! But was the dropping of the patronymic name the action of a bored son – or an irate one? Had Louis discovered the truth of his actual parentage, and feeling confused and deceived, fallen out with his adoptive father, Uncle Willie?

There is the belief in the Scots branch of the Thomsons of a serious financial disagreement with Uncle Willie causing Louis to be disinherited by his father. Cousin Bruce Thomson, the sole remaining Thomson in Crathie, along with his wife Alicia, knew Louis well: as an eleven-year-old, he had spent a year in France with Louis' son Max, a respiratory physician. Bruce had been sent there with suspected tuberculosis.

Cousins Alicia and Bruce Thomson in their Knock Art Gallery, Crathie, Aberdeenshire, with the author © J T Statham, 2018

Furthermore, coming from a large and modest Aberdeenshire family Uncle Willie would not have been used to the largesse of Louis' benefactress Princess Louise. Louis was cushioned. Alicia Thomson poses the following interesting question: was Louis' illegitimate birth and existence an inconvenience to the British royals? Was he made an offer to leave the UK he couldn't refuse? Whatever the cause of his departure, and despite speaking to surviving relations who knew him well, it remains shrouded in mystery and open to speculation.

One wonders if there are a few red herrings swimming around here. I would be very surprised if someone somewhere did not know the actual reason for his departure and the truth of his parentage. At the very least there should be documentary evidence but, in spite of my best efforts to find it, so far I have been unsuccessful. Access to his elusive birth certificate would shed some light on the situation, as would DNA tests. In any event Louis took off for France where he spent the rest of his eventful life. But he retained his British citizenship and, after a temporary breach, remained in close contact with his Scottish family. It seems he made up with his father: in 1926, in a letter from Kensington Palace to his Crathie postmaster brother Albert, Uncle Willie says 'we expect Louis to come over soon for a few day'.[13] Louis would periodically visit London to collect Cairn terriers from Bruce Thomson's father, Gordon.

But to return to the war: Unlike our two other protagonists this enigmatic forebear's life did not end in wartime tragedy. Louis Thomson was fortunate that he survived to enjoy a long and fulfilling life after the war, and left behind a large French family. As a well-connected figure brought up in a family of Jacobite origins, he was to continue to engage on the global stage as an international mediator later in the twentieth century. But at a time of tense international relations before the commencement of the First World War, was there a more curious reason for his abrupt departure from a cushioned existence in London? Was this bilingual, unusually well connected and highly educated Franco-Scot a potential asset to the authorities? Why did he move from an affluent quarter of London to a provincial and in many ways primitive French town? What explains the actions of this enigmatic medic? In spite of the various familial theories, other aspects of the man too, particularly his response to the horrors of war, remain puzzling to me. And to continue the intrigue, when settled in Burgundy as a country doctor after World War One, *Der ausländische Arzt*, the foreign doctor with perfect English, was to become of interest to the occupying Germans some years later, during World War Two. Bruce Thomson describes him as politically active 'in a maverick, loner sort of way'. He was also very influential locally. I ask myself did he play a role in the Resistance? The Germans were highly suspicious of him and interrogated him every night. He was later awarded both the *Croix de Guerre* and the *Legion d'honneur* by the French government. Was there a connection?

Jean Marie Bordelais with her parents and sister

Funded by his benefactress, Princess Louise, Louis studied medicine at St Mary's Hospital, London, gaining membership of the

Royal College of Surgeons in England in 1903, the Royal College of Physicians of London in 1903, and M D Lyons in 1908. In 1909 his registered address was still Laburnum Cottage, Kensington Palace. In 1910 it was Etrochey, la Côte-d'Or, Burgundy.

Before leaving for his country practice in Burgundy, Louis worked as a general practitioner in Lewisham in southeast London.

Madame Aline Thomson, Louis' daughter-in-law and wife of Louis' son, Jean, recalls his kindness, how he welcomed her into the family, and how committed he was to his patients in France. The good doctor did not charge patients who lacked financial resources in those pre-health service days. Later, little strips of Burgundy would be bequeathed to him in wills. Madame Thomson also commented that her father-in-law was proud of his Scottish origins. And he was apparently a fine water-colourist, but I have not at the time of writing been able to view his paintings. Bruce Thomson comments that 'It was an awfully long time ago that I saw Louis' watercolours, but I thought they were quite brilliant. He was a real enthusiast, and used to take me in his old Peugeot and plant me on a stool, fully equipped to paint the landscapes and old stone buildings that appealed to him.' Louis' appreciation of the stunning beauty of Serbia and Montenegro shines through his writings; visual memories to be stored away for later inspiration.

PREVENTION IS BETTER THAN CURE[14]

After the war and living in the Côte-d'Or, not far from Dijon, Dr Thomson was ahead of his time as an exponent of public health, unlike the Côte-d'Azur tuberculosis doctors of the late eighteenth century. He had survived war conditions in Serbia in some of the worst public health challenges imaginable, and looked after sufferers in one of the worst epidemics in history, the typhus epidemic, not to mention those suffering from typhoid, cholera, malaria and dysentery. These experiences would have made an indelible mark on him and his wife, who was later to engage with prominent twentieth-century political and intellectual figures.

Louis Thomson was a great believer in preventative medicine. Perhaps influenced by his Scots forebears' partiality to a dram, he was prone to comment in his book about the amount of alcohol he observed consumed in Serbia, 'raki, the curse of Serbia'. It is not known if he would later advise his patients in Burgundy about the perils of wine. In any event he instituted a number of social reforms and public health initiatives there after the war. He addressed the dismal state of housing in Châtillon where he lived, ridding the town of slums and instigating a house-building programme. He eventually lived at one of his constructions, at No 1 de la rue Louis Pasteur, named in honour of the great French microbiologist; another street was named after French physiologist, Claude Bernard, mastermind of blind research and also of the concept of homeostasis, the physiological mechanism that maintains equilibrium in the body. Alas there was no 'rue Hunter' nor a 'rue Fleming'. (John Hunter was a celebrated surgeon and his brother William an influential anatomist; Fleming was the inventor of penicillin; the discovery took place at Louis' alma mater, St Mary's Hospital, London, in 1928.) Dr Thomson also introduced other important public health initiatives in Châtillon-sur-Seine, such as running drinking water and electricity.[15]

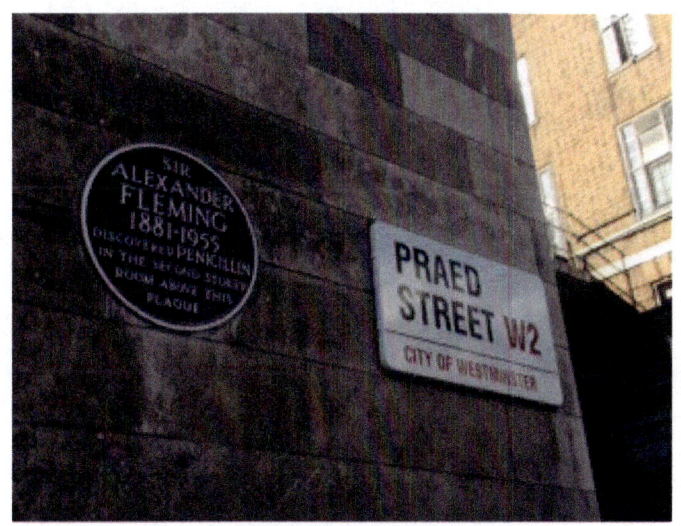

St Mary's Hospital, London

According to his daughter-in-law Aline Thomson, this doctor from overseas cut quite a dash in the traditional, provincial Burgundy town, engaging socially and forming a tennis club. Aline's son, Jean-Max Thomson, who was quite young when his grandfather died, describes his *Bon-Papa* as a Victorian eccentric. The debonair doctor was at the very least a character and an individualist.

Louis Thomson in Étrochey between 1912 and 1914 with his De Dion-Bouton type DN, which he took to Serbia. The car was later abandoned in Prizen

THE WAR DOCTOR

But to return to the First World War, and specifically to the Balkans, in early 1915 Dr Thomson had responded to an appeal for help with the French war effort in Serbia. He was at the time chief army medical officer to the French army's 27th Infantry Regiment, based in a temporary hospital in Dijon, as well as covering two other hospitals. Time hung heavily on his hands. Like his namesake cousin, Louis Middleton, the young medic was keen to engage in the war, although he wasn't quite sure in what capacity. He had a desire to see, to try, to do – but what?[16] This older Louis however was already qualified and established as a practising doctor, unlike his younger Middleton medical student cousin.

The answer came one Sunday afternoon: as Dr Thomson was finishing his ward round, a secretary came in with a ministerial dispatch seeking medical volunteers to help combat an outbreak of typhus in Serbia.[17]

SERBIA

Austria had declared war on Serbia on 28 July 1914, following the assassination by *Mlada Bosna* of Archduke Franz Ferdinand of Austria and his wife Sophie, Duchess of Hohenberg. The *Malda Bosna* or Young Bosnia, were a revolutionary group of young Bosnian Serbs, Bosniaks and Bosnian Croats. Their ideologies included unification into Yugoslavia and Pan-Serbianism. The date of 28 June was significant, coinciding with the First Battle of Kosovo on 28 June 1389 when Serbia was defeated by the Turks.

Negotiations following this had been unsuccessful. National military forces had already been gathering, and the incident in Sarajevo ignited an international conflagration, the likes of which had never been seen before. The Austrians were ruthless in reprisal, which was enacted on the entire Serbian population.

The major European powers grouped into opposing camps and focused their interest on the Western Front, the Dardanelles, the

Middle East and North Africa. The Serbs' allies were dilatory in their assistance to the Serbian nation, to say the least. The Serb army held up valiantly against the Austrians – but they were worn out by 1915 (and indeed had been even before 1914, following the Balkan wars).

In April 1915, having responded to the appeal for medical volunteers, Louis and his wife Jean Marie Bordelais left France for Serbia to a scenario of advancing armies and a terrible typhus epidemic. Louis' wife had not wanted him to go, and thought the better of letting her dashing young husband venture forth alone; she eventually agreed on condition that she accompany him. By October of that year they had joined the Serbs in their retreat to the Adriatic coast. In his book *La Retraite de Serbie*,[18] Louis Thomson addresses these two harrowing episodes: firstly the devastating typhus epidemic, and then the gruelling exodus over the high winter mountains of Montenegro and Albania.

THE TYPHUS EPIDEMIC

The Serbian army had only four hundred doctors for over half a million personnel. Like the rest of the population Serb doctors had been struck down by war and disease. In addition to the terrible typhus epidemic and the war-wounded, Louis Thomson was to face typhoid, cholera, dysentery, tuberculosis, diptheria, scarlet fever and malaria – and severe food shortages. The Serbian government had appealed for medical help from allied governments and French, Russian, Swiss and Greek medical workers and missions rallied to their aid. But the most significant foreign mission that came to the aid of the Serbs, which the Serbs honour and remember to this day, was the Scottish Women's Hospitals for Foreign Service (SWH).

Curiously the Franco-Scots Dr Thomson, of the French medical mission, does not mention these valiant Scotswomen in his book. He was in the Kragujevac area on 26 October 1915 where the SWH had been based. He refers to women doctors and nurses from the English Stobart's Mission, organised by Mabel Stobart, from Dorset, and other English nurses and doctors, and to Lady Paget, but never the SWH.

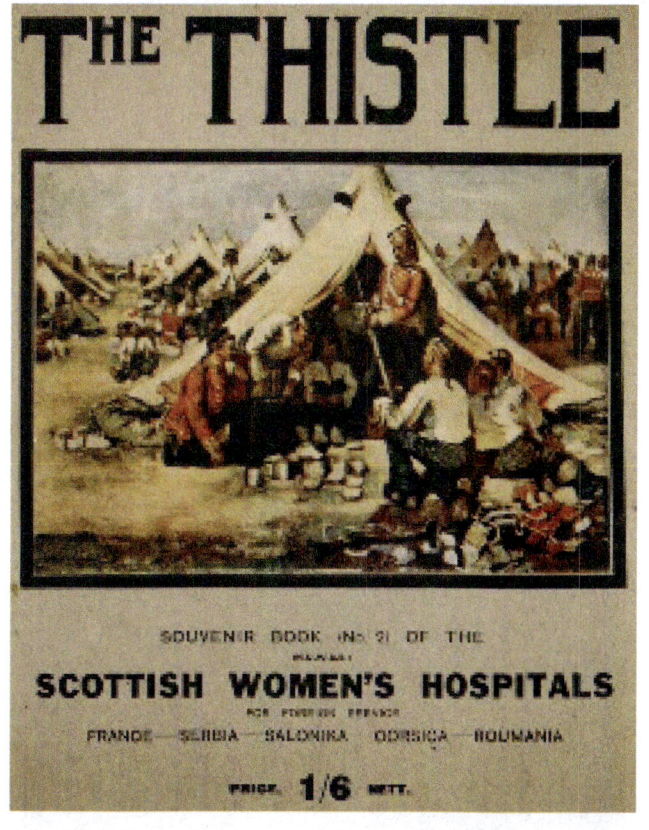

THE SCOTTISH WOMEN'S HOSPITALS
FOR FOREIGN SERVICE

THE THISTLE

SOUVENIR BOOK No. 2 OF THE
SCOTTISH WOMEN'S HOSPITALS
FOR FOREIGN SERVICE
FRANCE — SERBIA — SALONIKA — ODESSA — ROUMANIA

PRICE **1/6** NETT

Many celebrated Scots women doctors and nurses had cared for Serbia's typhus sufferers in early 1915. These included Dr Elizabeth Ross from Tain, who sadly succumbed to typhus, and died in the Kragujevac Military Hospital on 14 February 1915. She is still remembered there every year on the anniversary of her death. Also in Kragujevac had been Glasgow graduate Dr Katherine MacPhail.[19] In June 1915, she too contracted the highly infectious disease, but mercifully recovered, although her hearing was permanently impaired.[20]

For myself, as a Scottish woman health professional, the SWH resonates. The descriptions of the conditions they endured fill in some curious gaps that I found in Uncle Louis' book, especially in the earlier part. He describes his book as recorded notes with no attempt at literary merit and, significantly, that he had chosen not to record medical details. It is to other sources, like accounts of the SWH, that I have turned to learn about the dire situation Louis Thomson endured, and in which he seemed to have thrived.

The Scottish Women's Hospitals was founded in Edinburgh by Dr Elsie Inglis and funded by the National Union of Women's Suffrage Societies (NUWSS). The SWH were pioneering Scottish women doctors and nurses who couldn't get standard medical and surgical posts in Scotland; it was assumed in those days that missionary work was the appropriate role for these dedicated and highly skilled professional women.

Dr Elsie Inglis, founder of the Scottish Women's Hospitals

Their war background was that early in the war, in 1914, Dr Inglis offered the SWH's services to the Royal Army Medical Corps. Their unceremonial response was:

Go home and sit still woman. [21]

But these pukka boys in khaki hadn't reckoned on Scottish women's determination. Coming from generations of Scots women doctors and nurses, I can attest to this immutable force. With neither fuss nor fanfare these modest, matter-of-fact women got on with the job, crossing the Channel and offering their services to the French, Belgian and Serbian authorities who were more grateful in their response and gracious in their appreciation.[22]

The Scottish Women's Hospitals for Foreign Service

By the end of 1914, the SWH had organised a hospital in Calais for the Belgian army; then another at Royaumont, which ran throughout the duration of the war under the direction of the French Red Cross. Others were opened in Troyes and Villers-Cotterets. These busy Scotswomen set up field hospitals, fever hospitals, dressing stations and clinics in France, Salonika – and in Serbia.

> *The Serbians very much admire the work of the Scottish Woman, their economy (every penny does the work of two) their personality and bearing. The officers speak of them with the utmost respect and the soldiers, admiring their trim grey uniforms and rapid walk, call them affectionately the 'little grey partridges'.*[23]

Moving swiftly on from the avian nomenclature, I am well acquainted with the likely hive of activity that would have been generated around these *perjink* professionals: it was my cradle.

In Serbia the SWH were funded and supported by, amongst others, avuncular Glasgow grocer and tea magnate, Sir Thomas Lipton, sometime resident of the Cap Martin Hotel. This *gallus* Glaswegian from the Gorbals was a keen sailor and would courageously sail supplies down the Corinth Canal for his doughty compatriots, dodging mines, submarines and Zeppelins in his yacht *Eren*.[24]

Teabag branding celebrating the tea magnate and philanthropist Sir Thomas Lipton

There were other British missions: the Berry Mission and, as previously mentioned, the Stobart Field Hospital, as well as Lady Paget's mission. In his book,[25] Dr Thomson often refers to Lady Paget, wife of the British Ambassador in Belgrade.

Later, at the end of the Second World War, Lady Paget helped set up the Serbian Orthodox Church in Lancaster Road, London. The main beneficiaries initially were the Chetniks, the Royalists who left the former Yugoslavia after General Tito's Communists took over.[26] It was rather extraordinary for me, having just read about the valiant lady in *La Retraite de Serbie,* my uncle's book of a hundred years ago,[27] to walk into the Serbian Community Centre in 2017 to find the dining room named 'Lady Paget Hall'!

Lady Paget Hall, in the Serbian Community Centre, London W11

Oddly, there is no mention at all of Scots doctor Elsie Inglis in my uncle's book. The Scottish Women's Hospitals would undoubtedly have registered with the émigré Franco-Scots doctor. His allegiance by then seems to have been fully of the Gallic persuasion, although his daughter-in-law reported to me how proud he was of his Scottish origins. He never in fact took up French citizenship and always retained British nationality.

Interestingly, Jean-Max Thomson (Louis' grandson) named his third daughter (born in 2014) Elsie in recognition of her Scottish heritage. Jean-Max has no recollection however of hearing this name at his grandfather's knee. It is not a particularly common name in Scotland these days, far less France. His fourth daughter, born in 2017, was named Loïs. Was this a feminine derivative of Louis? 'Probably not etymologically, but that's why we chose it, in part!' says Jean-Max.

But the foreign medical missions from whatever country had a massive challenge on their hands in 1914–15. The situation in Serbia was dire. By December 1914, over 170,000 Serb soldiers had been killed, wounded, were ill or missing. The Serbian army had managed however to repel three successive Austro-Hungarian invasions, and the Serbs had taken a large number of Austro-Hungarian prisoners-of-war, estimated to be 40,000. At the end of 1914, Valjevo (about fifty miles southwest of Belgrade) was considered to be the epicentre of the typhus epidemic. At the beginning of 1915 there were thought to be about 500,000 people infected, with a mortality rate of forty per cent in this, the worst typhus epidemic in history. These prisoners-of-war had no immunity and were dispersed as farmhands throughout Serbia, and this is thought to have been a contributary factor in spreading the infection. The cause of the epidemic was little understood at the time, but subsequently found to be spread by body lice. Louis and his wife cannily elected to travel to Serbia by car, in order to avoid exposure to the disease in trains.

Dr Thomson wrote that he would not go into clinical detail, and his book leaves much to the imagination. A hundred years later, at the time of writing, in an age of television and social media, explicit violent visual detail is the order of the day. A century ago the good Franco-Scots doctor saw no reason to subject his readers to the horrors of amputations, gangrene, fearful diseases and the like; he also didn't see fit to detail the ordeals he and his wife, who assisted him clinically, would have endured in Chabats, his first port-of-call. His reticence was slightly less in the retreat.

His documentary account owes something to being partly a travelogue, with notes possibly hastily written in challenging conditions, as well as employing the traditional medical method of recording observed clinical signs (in this case applied to events rather than disease) – but not the writer's personal emotional response. The good doctor, it would appear, sought to spare his readership. This has long been the way in this profession,[28] and especially in those post-Victorian times. The emotional cost to the doctor and his wife can only be guessed at; it is not clear to me how this plucky pair bore their ordeals. I have had to turn to other sources to learn more about the conditions they would have endured.[29]

Louise Miller, in writing about Flora Sandes, an Englishwoman who fought in the Serbian army, recounts that the Scottish Women's Hospitals were the most noteworthy and significant of the foreign medical missions in Serbia. She quotes from Dr Elizabeth Ross' description of the conditions she found in January 1915 at the First Reserve Hospital in Kragujevac, where the Anglo-American Unit had previously been based:

> *I have seen some of the worst slum dwellings one can find in Britain, but never anything to approach these wards in filth and squalor. Men lay crowded together on mattresses. We saw three shivering together on two mattresses. No one washes them; they lie in the weakness of fever, becoming filthier and filthier. When a man dies the next comer is put straight onto the same dirty mattress, between the same loathsome sheets. The place is full of orderlies certainly, but they crouch apathetically in corners, waiting their own turn to die.[30]*

Dimitrije Antić, the director of the hospital where Dr Elizabeth Ross worked, left this account of the Scottish doctor's Serbian experience:

> *It is my duty, and the place is right, to mention with great respect the name of a foreign colleague from Scotland, Miss Elizabeth Ross, who came to help as a volunteer in the most difficult moments for my hospital. She tirelessly treated soldiers sick with typhus, fearless for her life, day and night. Everyone around*

her was falling down with typhus; she saw that very well and she was aware that the same destiny awaited her; but, despite my appeals and warnings to look after herself, she heroically performed her grave and noble duty till the end. Unfortunately, the inevitable came quickly: Miss Ross contracted typhus. She was even more courageous in sickness: severely ill, she lay quietly in her bed in a very modest hospital ward. Her only complaint was that she couldn't provide medical assistance any longer to our sick soldiers! Indeed, one of the rare shining examples of medical sacrifice. She is buried in Kragujevac town cemetery.

Upon hearing the news of her death in Serbia, the residents of her home town of Tain in Ross-shire raised funds for the memorial 'Dr Elizabeth Ross Bed' at the Kragujevac Military Hospital, and for surgical and medical needs in Serbia. The Serbian daily Samouprava *informed its readers how Dr Ross managed six wards in the hospital without nurses, relying solely on the help of hospital orderlies. 'There was no wood for cooking or for heating, something was always missing; one day there was no bread, another there were no eggs or milk and so on.'*

On the day of her funeral service all local stores were closed and large numbers of the people of Kragujevac came out to pay their respects. The tradition of respect has been kept alive to the present day. Each year on 14 February at noon Kragujevac remembers Dr Elizabeth Ross.[31]

I can attest to the respect accorded to the foreign medical missions in World War One, and to the Scottish Women's Hospitals in particular, by the immense gratitude and appreciation that has been shown to me, a hundred years later, at several *pomen* (memorial services) at St Sava's, the Serbian Orthodox Church in Notting Hill, London, where I live.

I had done nothing to afford myself of such appreciation other than being related to Dr Louis Thomson of the French Medical Mission in Serbia; also I am a Scottish woman health professional, daughter of a Scots woman doctor, and granddaughter and niece of Scottish women nurses. None of my immediate female forebears, however, served in the war medical missions.

Pomen at St Sava's Serbian Orthodox Church, London, commemorating the centenary of the death of Dr Elsie Inglis, 26 November 2017 © Olga Stanojlovic, 2017

Descendants of Dr Elsie Inglis, St Sava's Serbian Orthodox Church, London

It was indeed humbling to be afforded such warmth and such a welcome. The deep appreciation felt by the Serbs for the contribution of these foreign medical missions was palpable. I was invited to two very special and poignant occasions honouring these brave women, one to mark the centenary of the death of Dr Elsie Inglis on 26 November 2017, and another, their fourth Memorial Service for Women in Foreign Medical Missions, on 25 February 2018. One of the speakers, Ailsa Clarke, outlined the hospitality experienced by these Scottish Women Doctors when in Serbia. I was fortuntate to be the beneficiary of Serbian hospitality a hundred years later.

Serbian folk dancers at an event celebrating women in foreign missions, Lady Paget Hall, Serbian Community Centre, London, 25 February 2018

LA BEJANIA

In the dark times will there also be singing? Bertolt Brecht [32]

Louis Thomson had been working in Chabats in the north of Serbia from April 1915. He reports that by the autumn the life-threatening epidemics were over. The Serbs' horizon, however was darkening with threats of another order: the advancing Austro-German armies were approaching from the north. Chabats had suffered frequent episodes of Austrian aggression – there was a major bombardment on 24 September – and there was the additional fear of a Bulgarian invasion from the south. The opposing armies were closing in and the

Austrians had shown themselves to be in no mood for mercy. With these encroaching threats the people of Chabats were already evacuating their town towards the end of September.

Dr Thomson had to move his patients out of the hospital where he was based; at the same time more casualties were arriving from surrounding areas. On 14 October it was rumoured that the Bulgarians had occupied nearby Belgrade, and that the Greeks had blockaded the passage of British and French troops from Salonika. The Serbian situation could not have been more perilous.

On 14 October, General Putnik, Field Marshal and Chief of the General Staff of the Serbian army, gave the order to the Serbs to depart for Albania. Two days later, at midnight, the Thomsons had a knock on the door and were told to be ready to leave at first light. Their survival was to be a race against time.

My uncle and aunt and their party left to proceed on what he referred to as the *bejania*. I understand that is more accurately written as the *bežanija*. The French editors of his recently re-released account of the great retreat[33] say the word *povlacenje* is the more accurate term, as was confirmed to me by a Serbian teacher[34]. Dr Thomson and his party made slow and painful progress. He had hoped to continue contributing to the French medical mission when he reached his destination; at that stage it was not clear where that would be.

There were several possibilities of exit, and they travelled by a more northerly route, from Chabats via Valievo, towards Gornai Milanovats. They crawled along amongst a winding convoy of beleaguered people together with horses and oxen that struggled in the mud. He had hoped that the retreat would end in Gornai Milanovats, but in the face of further threats from the southwest they were instructed to keep going and to head towards Kragouyevats. Their tired horses hindered progress. By the time they got to Kragouyevats they had met some Englishwomen from the Stobarts mission who were evacuating their hospitals.

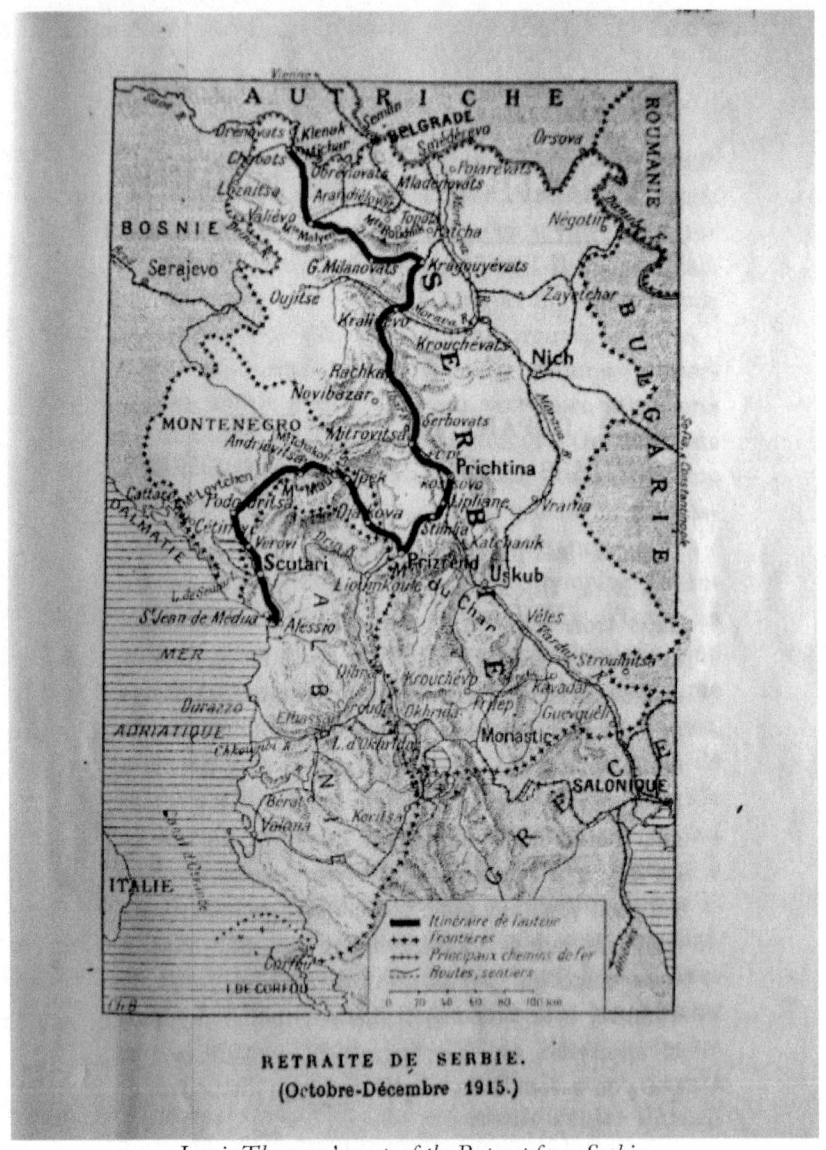

*Louis Thomson's map of the Retreat from Serbia,
from Chabats to St Jean du Medua*

They then heard that the Austrians had reached Valievo and they were therefore cut off from the French troops. The options for safe escape were narrowing further. Ploughing on through an endless mud bath in the direction of Kralievo, they got stuck, again and again, and were pulled out by oxen; another time Austrian prisoners-of-war dragged their car from the mud. They stayed in Kralievo in a hospitable peasant family home with earthen floors, a couple of three-legged chairs, and a fireplace where smoke escaped through the roof; harvested corn hung from the beams. After arriving in Kralievo, having passed streams of starving wounded evacuees, Louis remarked that the view from the town of Kralievo was one of the most beautiful he had ever seen. Apart from an episode of lumbago, his health seems to have held up well against the rigours of the journey. The march was lifted from time to time by evocative musical scenes, with Serbian soldiers following a gypsy violinist, reminiscent of pipers leading the Scottish regiments. The marching Serb army, he notes, visibly stiffened when passing an officer.

By 28 October refugees were pouring in to Kralievo, the Serbs still full of optimism for the future. Uncle Louis remarks how they drank endless cups of tea – and still sang. But the Bulgarians had advanced upon Uskub and the Serb options were in fact diminishing. They were ordered to make their way to Rachka. The Thomson party again stayed in the modest dwellings of local peasants. He commented that in Rachka he was offered raki that he describes as 'the scourge of Serbia'. And so their procession proceeded, ploughing through endless mud and finding food and shelter when and where they could.

Louis noted worryingly that the population leaving Chabats had mostly concluded their journey at Valievo – especially women, children and the elderly – and to an uncertain end. From Kralievo the majority of refugees were rich families fleeing by car; the wounded and soldier recruits proceeded by foot. From time to time someone would burst into song with a Serbian lament, and the rest would join in.

From Rachka, Louis went on an outing to Novibazar, and there he recalls feeling a wondrous sense of being in the east for the first time, a feeling of awe that I can recall from my own travels in that corner of the world. He was transfixed by the Albanians in their richly embroidered clothes, women with veils, young girls in wide baggy trousers and men wearing the fez. He struggled more and more to find food; it was especially difficult to find oats for their weary horses.

En route to Motrovitza his car got stuck in water. Carts too were stuck, and he observed how vigorously horses were beaten until they moved. He often saw horses die under such duress. Again, however, he comments on how much he enjoys the scenery.

And so the pattern of the first leg of their wet, muddy journey was set. From Rachka they trudged through to Mitrovitsa and so to Pristina, where he prophesies that the destiny of Serbia would be played out again on the plains of Kosovo. On 11 November 1915 they were ordered to leave for Prizrend. An ordeal of alpine proportions awaited them.

Louis was enchanted by Prizrend – under snow it was like a fairytale. On 19 November they were ordered to leave by the mountains. In the guise of gifts for their Serbian hosts they disencumbered themselves and their horses of much of their baggage, even leaving behind his beloved car. They progressed towards Montenegro with foreboding. From Ipek they braced themselves for looming black mountains and entered foaming gorges. Their first ascent was to Tchakor at 2,000 metres. In spite of horses falling into the water and two dying, this whimsical man was still mesmerised by his surroundings; he describes the scene there as une vue féerique – fairyland. The paths were terrifyingly exposed and people suffered altitude sickness. Worse was still to come with snow blindness, wary locals, starvation and typhoid fever. And then they descended to Podgoritsa. Thoughout their exodus, blankets and clothes would disappear and sometimes reappear on the backs of fellow travellers.

Following the descent from what Louis describes as his 'winter wonderland', on 30 November they were ordered to march across the plain to Scutari. They were misdirected round the lake however and found themselves again surrounded by ravishing mountainous views. Their Adriatic destination awaited them with the promise of food, comfort and medical work.

Alas, it was not to be. The Austrians had blockaded the ports and the expected provisions had been sunk in the port of Saint-Jean-de-Medua, so the suffering of the starving Serbs and their travelling companions continued unabated. They heard how in Ipek an officer from the first army had thrown away his heavy cannons, and national songs were sung amongst the explosions and columns of rising smoke.

They arrived at Scutari on 4 December 1915. Gaunt Serbian soldiers poured in throughout December, weak, starving and debilitated. The roads were strewn with dead horses – and dead people. Amidst bombardment and starvation, the Serbs were coming to realise that their homeland was well and truly invaded. But when they approached the Adriatic, where they had thought their ordeals would be over, they found that the Austrians had blockaded the ports, thus cutting off the possibility of supplies coming in by sea.

On Christmas Eve, the spirits of Louis' party were raised by the Serbian refugees singing Romany songs. This transcendental musical moment lifted those starving souls, in one of the most desperate scenarios imaginable; their journey's end was so near, yet so far away. Having survived scaling freezing heights with inadequate provisions and enduring hunger and starvation, their trials were not yet over.

On Christmas Day, the weary fellow travellers were ordered to leave for Medua. The Thomsons and their Serbian companions, who had accompanied them from Chabats, then parted company, the Serbs leaving for a very uncertain future. In this last leg of their retreat, Louis' party passed ruins of houses destroyed in the Balkan war of 1912, and struggled through the last quagmire. A priest offered them wonderful hospitality that set them up for the last leg of their Balkan journey and finally they reached the Adriatic Sea, at Saint Jean-de-Medua.

On 6 January 1916, they were transported on the Italian ship Brindisi to Bari in Italy. In his book, Louis' Serbian swan song was an unusually personal revelation, a profound profession of regret that he had to leave his Serbian friends at a time of such desperate need.

OPANAKS AND OXEN

The World War One theme of mud and mire endured throughout this gruelling escape. The challenge to men, women and children, oxen, and again, the long-suffering beasts of burden in battle, the horses, was immense. The weather in the retreat was terrible, and the roads had had the benefit of neither a Thomas Telford, a Robert McAlpine, nor the French equivalent. Dr Louis Thomson reported that the road to Rachka was the first road they saw that could actually be called a road and that had been built by engineers.

He had travelled with his wife, a party of four Serbian, two drivers, an interpreter, a nurse and a little orphaned girl, Militza, who had been starving in Chabats (where he had supplied her and her *baba* [grandmother] with food provided by Lady Paget). Also with him was his beloved car, his Dion-Bouton type DN.

Dr and Madame Thomson, a little girl (I am guessing Militza) and his iconic De Dion-Bouton, a little the worse for wear

This car, his pride and joy, not surprisingly, lost some of its sparkle en route. Along with ox-carts it often had to be hauled out of the mud, which was sometimes five inches deep. He extols the virtues of his car's Michelin (not Dunlop) tyres. Sometimes the car had to be pushed uphill. Alas his car had to be abandoned on 19 November at Prizrend. He credits the ox-wagons, along with the *opanaks*, the traditional Serbian leather sandals, with facilitating the eventual escape to safety of the Serbs who managed the journey.

But the bad weather and poor roads had the effect of serving the Serbians too, as the Germans and Bulgarians could not deal with the severe winter conditions to advance past the Albanian mountains; thousands of Serbians avoided capture and eventually escaped to Corfu. The Serbians called the rain 'the little friend of Serbia': it saved practically the whole of Serbia's remaining army and populace. However, approximately 150,000 to 200,000 Serbs perished on this harrowing winter journey by foot. The Serbian army's retreat through Albania is considered by the Serbs to be one of the greatest tragedies in the history of their nation.

What is notable, however, is how in the face of the Four Horsemen of the Apocalypse, Louis Thomson devotes so much detail to the ordeals endured by his car, rather than himself, and his frequent comments on the beauty of the mountains and the charms of the little towns he finds on the way through this scenic part of the world. It would appear the experience was for him an adventure. Again, turning to author Louise Miller, a scene of a different order faced by the violin-carrying Flora Sandes is recorded: approaching a hut on a hillside she peered inside and found '... 9 dead Austrians, a horrible sight, the poor devils lay just as they died, from sickness and starvation, unable to go any farther.'[35]

As Louis Thomson said in his Foreword, 'Leave aside the personal element (in these notes) and you'll understand what the tragic exodus of an army and of a people was like.'

How I would have liked to read his 'personal element', over and above his description of the journey and the scenery! It would have been of interest to me to learn more about his motivation, his inspiration, his perspectives over and above his observations, and to understand more of his feelings about his experiences – and, for that matter, those of his wife. I have had to read between the lines, particularly about his time in Chabats, and seek background sources elsewhere. He seems however a little bit more open about his experiences on the Great Retreat, especially during the latter part in the mountains, perhaps because he was operating not so much as a doctor of medicine, but largely as an inexperienced mountaineer.

In this, the most harrowing journey imaginable, enduring freezing cold in a particularly cold winter, hunger and starvation, he seems enchanted by the surrounding scenery. In fact he comments on the fairytale landscape more than once. Amidst this ordeal, picturesque Balkan towns entrance him. Louis Thomson focuses on the beauty of an Albanian house, for example, with its garden of lemons and oranges, and he comments upon the exceptional hospitality of the Albanian hosts. He describes too the house owned by Lady Paget's husband, Sir Ralph Paget, as like a castle. He seems sustained and perhaps diverted by the surrounding scenery, and often lifts his eyes to the high mountains.

It is possible some of the intensity of experience is lost in translation. Louis was brought up by a Frenchwoman and an Aberdonian, his ostensible parents in London, and it is not clear to me which language was his actual mother tongue, French, English, or Doric for that matter. In spite of retaining his British citizenship he identifies as a Frenchman in his book. (...*nous autres Français*).[36] His book is written in French, and seems to have been aimed towards a French audience. (He would have been more than capable of writing it in English, too, but I have been unable to find any trace of an English edition. Why he didn't write an English edition remains unknown.)

It is not an easy task in any language for a relatively inexperienced writer to convey to the 'folks back home' extreme horror, as well as the breathtaking beauty of strange foreign lands. I had this experience myself having travelled in that beautiful Balkan part of the world, and also seen the pink Hindu Kush and the mighty Himalayas. I recall being astonished by the sheer beauty of these foreign mountainous lands, and I remember clearly my sense of frustration at feeling unable to convey adequately the beauty laid before me when writing to my family. At the same time human suffering not previously experienced was laid bare. There was a dilemma about how much misery to convey, and how much to spare the reader.

But the good doctor had noted earlier that he was not going to record medical details: perhaps this low-key approach to documenting a war doctor's extreme experience extends to the general suffering around him, although he does seem to get a little more exercised about the challenges crossing the high mountains of Montenegro in freezing Alpine conditions. They had to cross the Trechievik Pass at an altitude of 1,700 metres by foot; they couldn't mount their horses as the horses were too tired, weak and hungry. The march in that area was in fact torture. Their feet were cold and bleeding; some people developed frostbite and later had to suffer amputations in Scutari. Up and down the high mountains they trailed with their horses and oxen, as people slipped and slid on ice, and fell, wading through freezing streams in the valleys. Ascending these perilous icy slopes these untrained climbers of all ages and physical ability were required to employ the skills of experienced alpinists, cutting steps with axes. Evacuees and horses alike were blinded by snow.

Furthermore the locals in some remote, more lawless places were hostile and they struggled to get food and water from them. Louis comments that his worst memories were in the mountains of Tserna Gora where, on top of everything else, more and more people were succumbing to typhoid fever.

But it is notable how transfixed he was by the visual beauty around him, and that he was seemingly less exercised by the ordeals endured: perhaps this preserved him. And, unlike my other two uncles, he was not there to shoot and be shot at; his job as a doctor was to save life, and that was what he did. By comparison Louis Middleton went from learning about saving life at medical school to the ordeals of soldiering at the Somme.

UN CANDIDE EN CAMPAGNE[37]

Having survived the horrors of war, Louis picked up his medical duties again as a country doctor, and also engaged in social reform in Châtillon-sur-Seine where he lived. He had, however, acquired a taste for adventure not easily quieted, along with a sense of not having fully fulfilled his mission in Serbia. An air of mystery accompanied the rest of his life, and beyond.

Louis' book, *La Retraite de Serbie (Octobre–Décembre 1915)*, was re-edited and re-published in 2016 by three journalists, Jean-Arnault Derens, Laurent Geslin and Simon Rico who were also fascinated by this curious doctor's tale and interested in filling out the gaps in his story. Simon Rico writes of the quality of his writing and the precision of his travel notes; this arouses his curiosity about his background. They searched, but found little information in local archives where he had lived in Burgundy. They did discover in a newspaper article, however, that Louis Thomson had engaged on the international stage later in the twentieth century during the Algerian War. He had entered into negotiations in Geneva with Algerian politician and former World War One member of the French Army Medical Corps, Fehrat Abbas. Simon Rico ponders the question: was Major Thomson a secret agent? His fellow editor had referred to him as *le Major Thomson, un Candide en campagne*. It is not clear if the journalist, in referencing this philosophical tale by Voltaire, is unconsciously alluding to an illegitimate birth.[38]

Louis Leopold Arthur William Thomson died in 1969, aged eighty-nine. He had practised medicine for sixty-one years, which included his considerable contribution, along with his valiant wife, to the beleaguered Serbian nation, the epicentre of the First World War. Intrigue still surrounds him and arouses interest, and my research into the life of this second Great War Uncle Louis continues to raise questions. I shall continue to search for the so-far elusive answers and hope some day to complete his story.

Dr and Madame Thomson at home with daughter Yvonne © Bruce Thomson

REFERENCES

[1] *Camus, A (1957) L'etranger. Paris: Le livre de poche.*
[2] *Scott, W (2013) 'My native land' in The Complete Poetical Works of Sir Walter Scott. Charleston: Nabu Press.*
[3] *Thomson, LLA (1916) La Retraite de Serbie: (Octobre–Décembre 1915). Paris: Librairie Hachette.*

[4] Burns, R (2011) 'To a louse' in *The Complete Poems and Songs of Robert Burns*. Glasgow: Waverley Books.
[5] Thomson, LLA (1916)
[6] Burns, R (2011)
[7] Tolkien, JRR (2013) *The Hobbit*. London: HarperCollinsChildren'sBooks.
[8] Tolkien JRR (1995) *Lord of the Rings*. London: HarperCollins.
[9] Tolkien JRR (1995)
[10] Krippner, M (1980) *The Quality of Mercy: Women at War Serbia 1915–18*. Newton Abbot: David & Charles Publishers) Ltd.
[11] Thomson, LLA (1916)
[12] Thomson, LLA (1916)
[13] Thomson, W Letter to Albert Thomson, 21 February 1926.
[14] Derens, J-A, Geshin, L, Rico, S (2016) eds., re-publication of Thomson, LLA (1916). Paris: Non Lieu.
[15] Derens, J-A, Geshin, L, Rico, S (2016)
[16] Thomson, LLA (1916)
[17] Thomson, LLA (1916)
[18] Thomson, LLA (1916)
[19] Želimir D (2007) *Ever Yours Sincerely: The Life and Work of Dr Katherine S MacPhail*. Cambridge: Perfect Publishers Ltd.
[20] Želimir D (2007)
[21] http://scottishwomenshospitals.co.uk/ (Accessed 13 February 2017).
[22] http://scottishwomenshospitals.co.uk/ (Accessed 13 February 2017).
[23] 'Scottish Women in Serbia', *The Manchester Guardian* (1916) in Dixon, J (1988) *Little Grey Partridges: First World War Diary of Ishobel Ross who served with the Scottish Women's Hospitals unit in Serbia*. Aberdeen: The University Press.
[24] http://scottishwomenshospitals.co.uk/ (Accessed 13 February 2017).
[25] Thomson, LLA (1916)
[26] https://www.independent.co.uk/life-style/serbs-in-london-serbia-at-war-in-the-portobello-road-1077258.html / (Accessed 8 June 2018)
[27] Thomson, LLA (1916)
[28] Elton, C (2018) *Also Human: the Inner Lives of Doctors*. London: William Heinemann.
[29] Miller, L (2012) *A Fine Brother: The Life of Captain Flora Sandes*. London: Alma Books Ltd.
[30] Miller, L (2012)
[31] http://blogs.bl.uk/european/2016/02/serbia-celebrates-british-heroines-of-the-first-world-war.html. (Accessed 13 February 2017).

[32] Brecht, B https://gerryco23.wordpress.com/2016/12/31/in-the-dark-times-will-there-also-be-singing/
[33] Derens, J-A, Geshin, L, Rico, S (2016)
[34] With thanks to Zvezdana Popovic
[35] Miller, L (2012)
[36] Thomson, LLA (2016)
[37] Derens, J-A in Thomson, LLA (2016).
[38] Derens, J-A, Geshin, L, Rico, S (2016)

CHAPTER 8

INHERITANCE

When an inner situation is not made conscious, it happens outside as fate.
Carl Jung[1]

The wedding of Kate Chinn and Alexander Forbes

The closeness of two of the five Forbes brothers, James and Charles, is palpable in this family photograph, taken at the wedding of their brother Alex to Kate Chinn. My grandfather Charles Forbes, is on the extreme right with folded arms, and standing next to him is the kilted future Gordon Highlander, young James Clapperton. My grandfather would have felt protective towards his wee brother.

The loss of young James in 1915 was a terrible shock to Charlie and indeed to the whole Forbes family. In fact, Grandpa Forbes never got over the death of his younger brother. The feelings of my great-grandmother are unimaginable. The weight of my grandfather's burden was all-pervasive and endured throughout his life. Survivor guilt? Feeling he should have been there instead? Guilt at not protecting his younger brother? Or a never-ending untransmuted grief? We can but guess at the nature of his sorrow. My late mother confirmed not long before her death that her father's grief was overwhelming and enduring.

The unsupportable grief compromised my grandfather's mental health for the rest of his life. He suffered a manic depressive breakdown which reverberated throughout his years in what we now call bipolar disorder. He had talked of going out to Ypres to search for James, who was never found. I can recall my grandfather's fine black Rover car with its polished walnut dashboard and seats that smelled of their leather. I remember him driving it like a maniac. Mr Forbes' driving was the talk of the town in Portsoy, the former fishing village, where my grandparents spent their retirement years.

It was only in recent years, not long before my mother died, that I discovered that my insurance manager father withdrew the motor insurance from his father-in-law on account of his erratic driving. What a *stramash*. The fault lines in our family from this disagreement reverberated for half a century, with my grandfather devising a scheme whereby my mother, his only surviving child (his other daughter died in the Second World War), would not be his direct beneficiary following his death.

OTHER LEGACIES

The past is never dead. It's not even past.[2]

Charlie's other brothers, my great-uncles Alex and Newman, also farmers, were also plagued by depression, which included periods of hospitalisation. This grief, this insupportable anguish, carried on down through the generations, dulling with time into inchoate depression. I became an heir apparent; and the melancholy percolated down through other branches of the family too.

Forbes family grave, Portsoy Cemetry

Depression is predicted to be *the* major public health challenge of the future. The World Health Organisation (WHO) describes it as currently the third leading global burden of illness, and it is expected to be the leading cause of illness by 2030.[3] Recent research points to the inheritability of war trauma, how the psychological damage is passed down the generations. This refers to both overwhelming grief due to the loss of a loved one during war and to shell shock or post-traumatic stress disorder (PTSD).

There are many causes for depression, but I pose the following question: were the terrible two world wars of the twentieth century major contributing factors to this pervading emotional malaise? If depression and post-traumatic trauma may be inherited, the descendants of the war-bereaved and the war-traumatised have been bestowed an oppressive legacy. Professor of sociology Michael Roper has been instrumental in raising the profile of the suffering of the descendants of shell shocked combatants. In 'From the Shell Shocked Soldier to the Nervous Child: Psychoanalysis in the Aftermath of the First World War', Professor Roper writes that after the Second World

War second generation psychoanalysts like Anna Freud and Melanie Klein focused on the war within the child associated with that later war. Taking his historical focus back to the First World War Roper, with his concern for the descendants of traumatised combatants, traces the source of their malaise to their forebears' shell shock.[4]

The pain is transmuted emotionally from parent to child. An understanding of how psychological damage from war can pass down through families may be explored psycho-dynamically. Recent epigenetic research offers a different approach and an understanding for those of a scientific persuasion, outlining how depression may be transmitted at a cellular level. Epigenetics is the study of heritable changes in genes. Environmental stressors such as traumatic emotions alter noncoding DNA. Such affected DNA in a traumatised individual transfers information to the next generation's DNA, so passing on the effects of trauma. The effect of this is to prepare for life in an adverse environment like a war zone[5].

Rachel Yehuda is carrying out interesting work in epigenetics in New York. Yehuda, a professor of psychiatry and neuroscience, is a pioneer in the field of post-traumatic stress disorder (PTSD). Mark Wolynn, founder and director of the Family Constellation Institute, describes how Professor Yehuda has found evidence of pre-conceptual trauma with consequent epigenetic alterations affecting both parent and child. This offers an understanding at a genetic level of how serious psycho-physiological trauma is carried on down through the generations.[6] She has studied cortisol levels in the children of Holocaust survivors and controversially found it to be low – as with their parents. (It has often been thought to be high in stress.) These offspring are then predisposed to experience the PTSD symptoms of their parent. She had similar results in her trials with war veterans and with pregnant mothers who were at the site of the World Trade Centre attacks on 9/11.[7] It is thought that this adaptive process prepares the next generation to deal with the sort of trauma their parents had suffered. This is however a mixed blessing: one has the tools to respond to a stressful situation; on the other hand, an exaggerated startle response could be the result.[8] A preparedness to recoil in response to a bomb when an exhaust backfires may not be the best way to walk down the high street.

But whether these war-derived psychological traumata to families were generated by the nervous breakdown of the combatant, or due to the tragic loss of a loved one, the inheritability of psychological pain is finally being addressed, and by different disciplines. Various terms have been used to describe the trickle-down effect of psychological disturbance, such as Sigmund Freud's 'traumatic re-enactment' and 'repetition compulsion'. Freud suggests the point of this psychic process is an unconscious effort to repeat the issues until the matters may be resolved.[9]

More recent contributors to this field of understanding of war-related transgenerational trauma at an emotional level include professor of psychiatry Vamik D Volkan. Professor Volkan deduces from clinical analysis that 'Untold wars are not only present in the soldiers themselves; even after they leave the battlegrounds behind, such wars are kept alive in the next generation and often in those that follow.'[10] Professor Volkan has worked with Lord John Alderdice, who made a deep impression on me when I heard him speak about his work with brutalised young men in Northern Ireland. Talking cures were impossible due to lack of trust, especially when the patients did not know the religion of the professional. The only way the psychological professionals could get through to these traumatised, often sexually abused young paramilitaries, was with music. The key to communication was drumming.

Professor Volkan coins the concept 'transgenerational disposition'[11] by way of illustrating how psychological trauma is handed down. He elaborates with the notions of 'the telescoping of generations'[12] and 'ancestor syndrome'[13] in the case where the image of a lost child is 'deposited' onto subsequent children. Volkan goes on to say that this process is not a dissimilar phenomenon to Klein's 'projective identification'.[14] Depositing images, where a parent has lost a child and unconsciously deposits images of the dead child into a subsequent child, operates like 'psychological DNA'.[15]

The inherited wounded psyche is carried in the body, in speech and in family patterns and, as discussed above, the damage affects the DNA itself, and so is genetically passed down through families. Mark Wolynn writes how the answer to one's psychological problems may not be so much in our own stories, but in those of our parents, our grandparents or even our great-grandparents. How far back does one go? Wolynn outlines that recent research in neuroscience, cellular biology, developmental psychology and epigenetics stresses the importance of tracing at least three generations of family history to shed light on the aetiology of an individual's psychological suffering.[16]

UNSEEN BEQUESTS

Mine eyes do itch. Doth that bode weeping? William Shakespeare[17]

It is not clear how much my stoical mother was affected. She was prone to rubbing her eyes all her life, in the absence of any ophthalmological pathology. This brings to mind the *mise en scène* of the parting young Gordon Highlander with his shiny buttons dazzling my toddler mother saying 'Turn that bairns's face away'.

Eyes became a family theme as I entered the profession of orthoptics and my clinical experiences led me to query certain cases where children and also adults presented clinically with loss of vision but no found physical cause to account for this. This led me to research psychosomatic eye disorders at the Tavistock Clinic, and later to work towards developing a clinical treatment model, *The Mind's Eye Clinic*. I would, for example, see patients who had witnessed atrocities in war zones in the nineties – for example, in the Lebanon, Rwanda and the former Yugoslavia – in an eye out-patient department in a central London teaching hospital. The sufferers would arrive with symptoms suggestive of visual loss but no physical abnormality could be clinically found to account for the presenting sight problems. This had echoes of the clinical findings of pioneering ophthalmologist and psychoanalyst William Inman when he saw men sent over to Portsmouth from the Western Front with what I call 'shell blindness'. One such child I met who survived the war in the Lebanon stands out in the mind. She couldn't read the board at school in London, but no organic cause could be found to account for her difficulties. It became apparent that the child, her mother and their extended family had hidden in a cellar during the fighting.[18]

Psychologist Peter Heinl emphasises that the professional needs to tune into the mental world of the child at the time of the traumatic impact.[19] Whilst war trauma has caused untold suffering in my own family, it has by the same token sharpened my antennae to its prevalence elsewhere. It is interesting to note that that Mark Wolynn, author of *It Didn't Start with You,* set off on his journey of working with inherited family trauma with his own loss of vision. This cleared when he identified the familial genesis of his emotional and subsequent visual blocks.

In my own childhood the psycho-geographical route from my father's grief at the loss to all intents and purposes of his older brother's presence through severe shell shock, and at his father's subsequent death when my dad was still at school, was all unspoken. My father also lost one of his sisters in childbirth. I apparently look like the late Alice, and I am told I have aspects of my mother's late sister Nancy. To be reminded of their late sisters when they looked at me is a sobering thought. I wonder what they saw.

My father suffered from psoriasis for much of his life, and the psychological component of that disfiguring skin condition is well documented.[20] In spite of his sense of fun, ready humour and apt quote for any situation, my dad clearly bore a burden. As I have found at funerals, a glimpse is sometimes offered posthumously into the life of the deceased. At my father's funeral his former business assistant said to me 'Your father always worried about his brother.' Sadly my dad never shared this with me. Ever the conscientious parents, my mother and father would not have wanted to burden their offspring.

VISIONARIES?

Louis Thomson, of course, survived his war ordeals. He and his wife were fortunate to suffer neither disease nor injury in the desperate war conditions of beleaguered Serbia. How they survived emotionally through the typhus epidemic and the harrowing retreat is an interesting question. As well as good fortune, what sustained them? Black humour? Turning a blind eye? Unlike most men in war Louis Thomson had with him his life companion, his wife. In any event their experiences informed their later lives. Both were committed humanitarians. Madame Thomson engaged in intellectual pursuits and was a correspondent of French pacifist, writer and Nobel prizewinner, Romain Rolland. Rolland followed Eastern philosophy, including the works of Gandhi and Swami Vivekananda. He was also influenced by Jean-Jacques Rousseau, promoting the idea of a people's theatre, and writing a play about French revolutionary Danton[21]. Rolland created the notion of the 'oceanic feeling', later adopted by Sigmund Freud. On 5 December 1927, Rolland coined the phrase in a letter to Freud:

Mais j'aurais aimé à vous voir faire l'analyse du sentiment religieux spontané ou, plus exactement, de la sensation religieuse qui est ... le fait simple et direct de la sensation de l'Eternel (qui peut très bien n'être pas éternel, mais simplement sans bornes perceptibles, et comme océanique).
[But I would have liked to see you doing an analysis of spontaneous religious sentiment or, more exactly, of religious feeling, which is ... the simple and direct fact of the feeling of the 'eternal' (which can very well not be eternal, but simply without perceptible limits, and like oceanic, as it were).]

In his book *The Future of an Illusion* Freud ends with a discussion of the oceanic concept, and picks it up again in *Civilization and its Discontents*, where he responds to Rolland's request. He doesn't acknowledge Rolland, but credits the concept to an anonymous friend.

Aunt Jeannie, as she was known by Bruce Thomson, also apparently knew Joseph Stalin – in his younger, more idealistic phase, I hope.

The good doctor engaged socially as well as in social reform in Chattillon-sur-Seine. Not long after settling there he set up a tennis club. Post-war Louis Thomson was a committed social reformer. With the challenge of tuberculosis before the mid-1940s omnipresent, Louis was concerned with hygiene.[22] Having stayed in the most basic of dwellings in Serbia, and having to clear up mucky water to prevent the spread of malaria amongst other things would have made an indelible impression.[23] His visits to military hospitals in Rome just after the war further informed him.[24] The country doctor engaged in improving housing in Chatillon and introduced public water and electricity supplies.[25] He named the address of his own home *1 de la rue Louis Pasteur*. Pasteur had been one the visitors to Haldane's conference in 1913 as documented earlier, when Haldane had hoped for 'devoting ourselves to the great common purpose which make mankind far better than anything in the past'.

REFERENCES

[1] *Jung, CG (1959) Aion: Researches into the Phenomenology of the Self (Collected works of CG Jung). London: Routledge. Cited in Wolynn, M (2016) It Didn't Start with You. New York: Penguin Books.*

[2] *Faulkner, W (1996) Requiem for a Nun. London: Penguin Random House.*

[3] *http://www.who.int/mental_health/management/depression/wfmh_paper_depression_wmhd_2012.pdf. Searched 30 May 2018.*

[4] *Roper, M 'From the shell shocked soldier to the nervous child: psychoanalysis in the aftermath of the first world war', Psychoanalysis and History, 18 (1) pp 39–69.*

[5] *Wolynn (2016)*

[6] *Wolynn (2016)*

[7] *Wolynn (2016)*

[8] *Hales, CN & Barker, D (2001) 'The thrifty phenotype hypothesis' British Medical Bulletin 60 pp 5–20. Cited in Wolynn (2016).*

[9] *Wolynn (2016)*

[10] Volkan, VD (2004) *Animal Killer: Transmission of War Trauma from One Generation to the Next*. London: Karnac Books.
[11] Volkan (2004)
[12] Volkan (2004)
[13] Volkan (2004)
[14] Volkan (2004)
[15] Volkan (2004)
[16] Volkan (2004)
[17] Shakespeare, W (1958) *Othello. Act 4. Scene 3*. London: Spring Books.
[18] Middleton, EM, Sinason, MDA, and Davids, Z. (2007) 'Blurred vision due to psychosocial difficulties: a case series', *Eye*, 1–2 pp 316–7.
[19] Heinl, P (2001) *Splintered Innocence: an Intuitive Approached to Treating War Trauma*. London: Routledge
[20] Alexander, F (1987) *Psychosomatic medicine*. London: WW Norton & Co Ltd.
[21] Rolland, R (2016) *Danton: 3 Actes*. London: Forgotten Books.
[22] Rico, S (2016) in Thomson, LLA (1916). *La retraite de Serbie: (Octobre-Décembre 1915)* Paris: Non Lieu
[23] Thomson, LLA (1916) *La retraite de Serbie: (Octobre-Décembre 1915)* Paris: Librairie Hachette.
[24] Thomson, (LLAT) (1917) *Aperçu sur les hôpitaux militaires de Rome*. Paris: Hachette Livre BNF.
[25] Rico (2016)

CONCLUSION

*The dead spake together last night,
And each to the other said,
Why are we dead* Joseph Lee[1]

Blood Swept Lands and Seas of Red

I emerged from the London Underground one grey autumn day in 2014 - and was arrested by the overpowering sight of 888,246 ceramic poppies, each one representing someone who had died in the First World War. This remarkable art installation, 'Blood Swept Lands and Seas of Red', covering the former Tower of London moat, represented those lost from Britain and her empire: it marked a hundred years since the beginning of that war.

Some were critical that the installation did not include the commemorative flowers of other countries, like, for example, le Bleuet de France (the blue cornflower of France), or the *madeliefje*, the white daisy of Belgium or Germany's blue forget-me-not, the *vergissmeinnicht*, but the sheer volume of these poppies alone was as shocking a spectacle as I've seen.

At the close of the installation I bought two of those poppies. One remains on my balcony and I see it every day. I gave the other to cousins James and Frances Forbes, who had so generously afforded me access to the late Private James Clapperton Forbes' letters, photos and medals, that they have so carefully tended. James C Forbes was the great uncle of both my second cousin, James Forbes, and myself. James, the last surviving Forbes farmer, grows, amongst other things, the barley for Caorunn Gin.

My ceramic poppy reminds me how the impressions of these three brave family men entered my life. The poppy installation, and how it captured the public imagination, evoked how the First World War had calibrated the national mood for a century. The emotional fall-out from that most terrible of wars extended far, deep and wide, and many families, like my own, were ill equipped to deal with the ensuing trauma and loss, which I have attempted to outline in my book. As my cousin, Alasdair McKichan, in Canada, who knew Uncle Louis (Middleton) said after reading this book, 'What awful fates so many of that generation suffered. I believe our aunt and my step-mother, Maisie, never really got over what happened to her beloved brother, Louis, and of course the same was true for our grandmother Middleton. The Forbes side of your family, as you suggest, was similarly affected.'[2] (To clarify, Alasdair's mother, Alice McKichan, née Middleton, died in childbirth, when Alasdair was born. Her widower, John McKichan, later married Alice's younger sister, our Auntie Maisie.)

I offer examples of the often tragic consequences of war in exploring its effect on one family. From these forays, I suggest that the war-faring demands made on young men merit serious questioning. Over the years, however, some have resisted the call to arms. As America was entering the First World War, some German-Americans and Irish-Americans contested being called up. There were conscientious objectors in the United Kingdom too, in both the First and Second World Wars, sometimes treated appallingly. A late friend, and eminent actor, endured an eye-opening spell in Wormwood Scrubs, until the old Queen Mary intervened. The anti-war movement however gained momentum during the Vietnam War, when the television age brought the reality of war into people's living room. This heralded massive attitudinal and social change in America and the west. I would add that I have met and befriended survivors of the Vietnam War and the Six Day (the Arab–Israeli) War and these men evidenced severe post-war psychological issues.

Many families, a century ago, carried on as best they could with their returning traumatised sons, or with the mind-numbing pain of their loss. They were weighed down with bewilderment caused by the cases of shell shock and sometimes the resulting stigma. Uncomprehending, and so often unaddressed and unresolved, the buried trauma and the paralysing grief were passed on to the following generations. I have come to see the lingering effects of the war reflected in my family and in thinking about these issues for this book, I have developed an enhanced respect for my late parents. I am aware of how they bore their war-generated pain with perhaps resignation - and certainly dignity, and managed their lives with courage, commitment to the family and humour. For myself, even after all these years of researching and writing about them, I still cannot describe the fates of Louis Middleton and James Forbes to others without choking up.

Uncle Louis Middleton's fate underpinned my commitment to psychosomatic eye disorders. Science developed in all manner of ways during the First World War - as it generally does in wars - with, for example, military and mechanical hardware, such as the tank. Chemistry was applied to the dark arts – the development of gases to kill - and by contrast, the creation of fertilisers by the same man. The advancement of surgery and medicine in war is also recognised too. The development of the understanding of the unconscious mind is a lasting and important legacy of this emotionally devastating war.

At the end of the nineteenth century, neurologists, physiologists, anthropologists and others were making early forays into the landscape of the psyche; seeds were being sown for the development of psychoanalysis. Pioneers like Jean-Martin Charcot and Pierre Janet, his student, and, from the German-speaking countries, Sigmund Freud, were excavating the deeper reaches of the mind in an effort to understand unexplained illnesses such as hysteria. The case studies at the Salpetrière Hospital in Paris initially were women; the German scholars in particular were resistant to the notion that men could suffer from hysteria. Charcot said 'it would be a red-letter day for him when he should meet with the condition (of hysteria) in a Prussian cuirassier'. This new way of thinking was largely held in suspicion by the more materialistic-minded British medical profession.

Shell shock in the early part of the twentieth century had the sufferers and families largely rendered helpless; many of the professionals' charges had short shrift in their care, and they could be locked away and forgotten. The fortunate few, like the poet-patients of Dr W H R Rivers at Craiglockhart Hospital, benefitted from this emerging discipline. Later, the Tavistock Clinic was set up – in 1920 - to understand the psychologically war-wounded. A hundred years later, hardly a radio programme about relationship problems or mental health issues gets mentioned without recommendations of therapy or mindfulness - and that was before the advent of Covid-19 in 2020, and the often solitary lockdowns, which brought challenges to mental health. Mercifully, however, the stigma of mental illness seems to be lessening its grip.

But to return to war, wouldn't life be simpler if humankind could resolve conflict constructively and not resort so quickly to military aggression? I recall my dismay and indeed utter astonishment when war was declared over the Falkland Islands in 1982. In 2018, the BBC Reith lectures – a series of lectures by someone considered eminent in their field – were on the subject of war. Canadian historian Margaret Macmillan delivered six broadcasts on the subject. Whilst comprehensive and informative, the very existence of war as an accepted institution was not, as I recall, challenged. Would six lectures on the subject of murder be considered a suitable subject for the Reith lectures? War, after all, is, amongst other things, institutionalised murder. I'd like to propose a series of Reith lectures on peace.

The more recent invasion of Ukraine in 2022 has been shocking, and raises more questions than answers about how to respond. Another bloodbath in Sudan dismays.

In spite of this story being dedicated to three family men, I have referenced the largely under-celebrated tale in Scotland, in my view, of the intrepid and inspirational women of the Scottish Women's Hospitals for Foreign Service. And by way of a postscript, I leave the last word to Nairn-born Mairi Chisholm: Mairi set off for Flanders with her friend Elsie Knocker in September 1914 to join the Flying Ambulance Corps in Belgium. Their task was to transport wounded soldiers to a field hospital in Fumes. They were dismayed by the sheer volume of men who died *en route* to these base hospitals. To address this delay in emergency care, they set up an unofficial dressing station a hundred yards from the trenches in an abandoned cellar in Pervyse, near Ypres. Later, these 'Madonnas of Pervyse' as they were called, were highly decorated, and awarded, amongst others, the Belgian Order of Leopold and the British Military Medal, and were made officers of the Most Venerable Order of the Hospital of St John of Jerusalem. Mairi was also honoured with the Order of Queen Elisabeth of Belgium and the 1914 Star. Mairi survived gassing twice.

Whilst making hot chocolate for the British men one day in the trenches, Mairi heard German spoken twenty yards away. Leaning over to the nearby German, Elsie said, *Eine schokolade?*

REFERENCES

[1] Lee, J (1917) *The green grass* IN *Ballads of battle*. London: John Murray.
[2] McKichan, A 30 August 2018.

GLOSSARY

Auld Reekie *(Scot)*	Edinburgh: referring to the stench in the smoky days of coal fires and before plumbing and sewage systems
belle époque *(Fr)*	beautiful era: referring to the time in France from the end of the Franco-Prussian War in 1871 to the beginning of the First World War in 1914; a period of artistic and scientific progress
birk *(Scot)*	birch
le Bleuet de France *(Fr)*	cornflower
bon viveur *(Fr)*	one who lives well; hedonist
Broch *(Scot orig Gael A' Bhruaich)*	Fraserburgh
byre *(Scot)*	cowshed
cette péninsule bénie des dieux *(Fr)*	this peninsula blessed by the gods
chiel *(Scot)*	fellow
commune *(Fr)*	town
couthie *(Scot)*	kind, cosy, sympathetic
cratur *(Scot)*	creature
crowlin *(Scot)*	crawling
dang *(Scot)*	damn
Deutchland über alles *(Ger)*	Germany above all else
drouthy *(Scot)*	thirsty
eine schokolade *(Ger)*	a hot chocolate
émigré *(Fr)*	emigrant
fechter *(Scot)*	fighter
ferlie *(Scot)*	marvel
gallus *(Scot)*	daring
hairst *(Scot)*	harvest
hibernants *(Fr)*	winter visitors

humlie *(Scot)*	cow without horns
kirk *(Scot)*	church; usually Church of Scotland
lad o' pairts *(Scot)*	a boy of humble origins who prospers academically in the open Scottish educational system
lave *(Scot)*	rest
loon *(Scot)*	boy
madeliefje *(Flemish Dutch)*	white daisy
moggan *(Scot)*	gaiter, or footless stocking. *Blue Mogganers* referred to natives of Peterhead
mucking *(Scot)*	clearing out manure
Nantaise *(Fr)*	from Nantes
neep *(Scot)*	turnip
onyway *(Scot)*	anyway
orthoptics	scientific profession ancillary to medicine specialising in the diagnosis and treatment of squint and other disorders of the extra-ocular muscles; also diagnostic work with endocrine disease; glaucoma and diabetes. From ortho *(Gr)* straight; optikos *(Gr)* eye.
perjinck *(Scot)*	near, smart, precise
plus ça change *(Fr)*	the more things change, the more they stay the same
pomen *(Serbian)*	commemoration
pour encourages les autres *(Fr)*	to 'encourage' others. Said ironically of an action (such as execution) carried out as a warning to others

poitrinaires *(Fr)*	those with chest infections
quinie *(Scot)*	girl
sod *(Scot)*	piece of turf
shell shock	term described by Charles Myers in *The Lancet* in 1915 to outline the breakdown of combatants in battle; variously described as war neurosis, combat stress, and later, post-traumatic stress disorder. Symptoms include shaking, nightmares, disturbed gait, loss of sight, speech or hearing. It is thought that the term was used in WW1 in spite of some of the sufferers never having been being near shell fire, rather than 'hysteria' (*Gr* hysterika = womb), to deny any suggestion of femininity.
séjour *(Fr)*	stay
stirk *(Scot)*	young cow (heifer or bullock)
stook *(Scot)*	sheaves of grain
stramash *(Scot)*	commotion, row, conflict
sojer *(Scot)*	soldier
scriever *(Scot)*	writer
stot *(Scot)*	bounce, rebound, stagger
tattie *(Scot)*	potato
vergissmeinnicht *(Ger)*	forget-me-not

ACKNOWLEDGEMENTS

Why did a quest for information about an unknown uncle become an all-consuming project that dominated the latter part of my life? I started writing this book during the period after the death of my mother in 2008. She had mentioned, only once or twice, great Uncle James' departure – without return – to the Western Front. The consequent depressive effect on my grandfather and descendants became apparent over more recent years.

Firstly, I pay tribute to my late parents, Mary Isobel Forbes and John Middleton. Both endured the two world wars of the 20th century and suffered great losses as outlined in this book. They bore their pain with equanimity. My mother's stoicism and my father's sense of duty were formidable. As characters, their strong sense of humour was a source of considerable joy for the family and their many friends.

Various events intensified my quest for information about the family losses of the First World War and focused my mind on the emotionality of this vast human tragedy. I was stopped in my tracks for example, when the mighty Sheena Wellington sang 'Hallowe'en' in her great Scots Song workshops at the Feis Rois festivals in Ullapool. 'Hallowe'en' is one of the most powerful songs about the First World War. It derived from a poem by Angus poet, Violet Jacob, about the loss of her son Harry at the Battle of the Somme.

Also, I had been aware of Louis Thomson who lived in France, although I had never met him. My aunt and my father had often spoken of him. I don't recall how I became aware of his great contribution to the sufferers of the terrible Typhus epidemic in Serbia in 1915, but I felt compelled to find out. What a rich vein of discovery was opened up! Learning about his successful mission in the war offered a ballast against the tragedies of my other two uncles, and opened up a valued friendship with my French cousins.

As I proceeded along my journey of enquiry a number of coincidences came my way. For example:

- I discovered that Charles Myers, who coined the term 'shell shock', had lived two doors away from where I now live.
- My brother had chosen to live in Dumfries, where Uncle Louis spent his last half century, though their stays did not overlap.
- When a medical student, my eldest nephew, now gynaecologist Gary Middleton, had his psychiatric placement at Louis Middleton's hospital, the Crichton Royal.
- My second nephew, architect Neil Middleton, had a summer holiday job in one of Uncle Louis' former wards, now commercial offices.
- When renting out our home as a holiday let, the management company awarded us a complementary holiday rental at le Golfe Bleu, in Roquebrune-Cap-Martin, on the Côte d'Azur. To my delight I discovered this holiday complex to be about 20 to 30 minutes' walk from the former Grand Hôtel du Cap, Uncle Louis' 'convalescent' home on Cap Martin.
- This Riviera holiday rental turned out also to be a stone's throw from the café where Uncle Louis would have eaten at night.
- I had a pre-arranged meeting with Monsieur Volpi. (I was put in touch with M Volpi by an old family friend and archivist from Nantes, Sylvaine Laffiché.) Jean Claude Volpi opened many doors for me. After taking me to a number of Uncle Louis's haunts, and having significantly expanded my First World War history of the area, I happened to quiz him about Robert Louis Stevenson who had sojourned in the nearby Menton when at a crossroads in his life. (Readers will have learnt of the significance of Robert Louis Stevenson in this family tale.) 'So you would like the Robert Louis Stevenson tour too?' he enquired! The next day I was taken on this engaging trip. M Volpi had researched and had been about to write a book about RLS when he was pipped at the post by Toulouse writer, Béatrice Balti, French author of Scottish

writers and other Scots of note, who had for some time been a Facebook friend of mine. (She had written about J M Barrie, Arthur Conan Doyle and William Wallace.)

- In the middle of the most intense research phase I was heading north to Aberdeenshire for a hillwalking holiday and by chance sent a communication to Frances Forbes, wife of my second cousin, James Forbes, asking if she might have any documents about great Uncle James Clapperton Forbes. Two weeks later I was sitting at their dining table in Banffshire reading great Uncle James' letters from Ypres. Thank you, Frances and James.
- We have a small plot in a community kitchen garden in land bequeathed to the community by Princess Louise. She is suggested in these pages to be the mother of cousin Louis Thomson.
- It transpired that the son of the pioneer of psychosomatic ophthalmology (William Inman) was the step-father of historian Professor Lucy Bland who has been so helpful to me.

Some would say that these coincidences suggested I was on the right tracks. Whatever interpretation may be made from this, I felt I was ploughing a fertile furrow.

Various family members have helped me: My brother, Andrew Middleton, former Dumfries resident, provided me with photographs of the Crichton. My four nephews, Gary, Neil, Ewan and Rory, contributed in different ways. Gary accompanied me on my first trip to the Crichton when a boy, and Neil passed on accurate information about the current use of one of Uncle Louis' former wards.

My cousin in Canada, retired lawyer Alasdair McKichan, who surely merits the status of family patriarch, is the only person I am aware of now who knew Uncle Louis. His memories of Louis Middleton's post-war quiet gentleness are poignant. Being older than me, Alasdair remembers the preceding generation's contemporaneous pain about Louis, in particular that of our late aunt, Maisie McKichan (née Mary Middleton) Uncle Louis' sister. I can recall Auntie Maisie referring to Louis as 'the flo'er of the flock'. (There were originally four siblings and she was more forthcoming about the horrors Louis endured than my father ever had been.) And as I have found in life, one often learns more about people after they have passed, than during their life: At my father's funeral, his former company assistant said that my father 'always worried about his brother'.

Cousins Bruce and the late Alicia Thomson of the Knock Gallery, Crathie, were unfailing in their generosity in providing information about Louis Thomson. Bruce had spent time with Louis Thomson when a boy in France. As the custodians of the Crathie Post Office and Thomson family archives they offered a treasure trove of family lore, photographs and documents, which they were only too happy to share. It was a shock when Alicia died far too young in January 2021 and before this book was completed.

by Louis Léopold Arthur William Thomson

It has been a joy to get to know the French side of the family better. Edith Thomson, who I met many years ago on a visit to Sainte-Chapelle in Paris, and possibly before at Crathie Post Office, enabled me to get in touch with her siblings. I reached out to her brother,

English teacher and author, Jean Max Thomson. Jean Max has been unstintingly generous in providing information about his late grandfather, and also in accessing more memories of Louis Thomson from his mother. His mother, Aline, died in 2022, before I finished this book, and before I had had an opportunity to meet her. I was fortunate however to have received an email from her where she charmingly outlined the kindness of her late father-in-law. I would like to thank also Jean Max's brother, Marc, for sharing one of their enigmatic grandfather's beautiful water colours, and also thank another brother, Georges, for a photograph.

Cousin Liz Hill in Devon, one of the many family Elizabeths, read the second draft, and made some pertinent suggestions, did a later proof read, as well as providing a copy of a portrait of Elizabeth Heslop, née Thomson, my great-grandmother and her great-great-grandmother. Elizabeth Thomson was cousin Louis Thomson's aunt and Uncle Louis Middleton's grandmother.

An unintended consequence of my research has been how it has rekindled connections with old friends. I attended numerous conferences and lectures about shell shock and the First World War between 2014 and 2018. Lucy Bland, Professor of Social and Cultural History at Anglia Ruskin University, Cambridge, was one such old friend I was delighted to meet again at a social history conference on shell shock. Lucy has since offered so much encouragement and recommended reading from her deep reservoir of historical knowledge.

At another conference I re-established contact with Fran Brearton, Professor of Modern Poetry at Queen's University Belfast. Fran had been an old friend of my husband. She, too, was most helpful in referring me to a colleague, Dr David Goldie at the University of Strathclyde, for information about Scottish war poetry. Dr Goldie was yet another academic unsparing in his generosity in providing information from his wealth of knowledge.

It was a pleasure at yet another conference about the First War, this time on poetry, to meet for the first time, fellow native of Broughty

Ferry, poet and psychiatric nurse, John Glenday. For the first time in my life I was able to share the experience of having a shell shocked uncle with someone else who had had this experience. John also expanded my knowledge of Scottish war poets.

And I have to acknowledge how important the inspiration was that was provided by the magnificent Jay Winter, the Charles J Stille Professor of History at Yale University, in a lecture at the British Academy on 9 July 2014. Professor Winter suggested that at least 25% of the combatants in the First World War suffered from psychological or neurological injury. Shell shock, he argued, arose from the monstrous character of the war itself. In a reception after his lecture Professor Winter kindly encouraged me to attend the following conference on shell shock and suggested how it could be possible at this fully booked event. This conference opened many doors to me.

Fellow orthoptist, Gillian Buchanan, neé Thomson (no relation), provided information from the history of Glasgow Eye Infirmary, our Orthoptic alma mater. This history had been written by her late father, Dr A M Wright Thomson, consultant ophthalmologist and one of our lecturers when studying orthoptics.

I owe an enormous linguistic debt of gratitude to Sue Bensassi in translating Louis Thomson's account of his time in Serbia. Judith Havas and Nina Hutchings also helped out linguistically, and French native, my cousin Jean Max Thomson, also rescued me from my rusty French.

The Gordon Highlanders' Museum provided information about Louis Middleton and James Forbes war histories from the Gordon Highlanders' war diary. A special acknowledgement has to go to the former Crichton Royal Museum archivist Morag Williams who has been most helpful in showing me the wards where Uncle Louis had whiled away his life. On a later visit she was able to provide documentation about him and I saw his case notes. My visits there were intensely emotionally demanding, but ultimately worthwhile. I perhaps unwisely opted at a later visit to stay in a hotel in one of the former Crichton Royal Hospital buildings, at the time of my third nephew, Ewan's, nearby wedding to Rebecca. I found the experience of a stay in the Crichton estate almost overwhelming. And I must thank too the Crichton Development Company Limited for enabling me to visit Grierson House, one of Uncle Louis' former wards, and now commercial offices.

The contribution of friends, acquaintances and colleagues has been heart-warming. My American friend, Gail Coles, who is a lecturer in cinema, was one of the first readers of the first draft and her warm encouragement has been pivotal. She also introduced me to her daughter-in-law, Leonora Meriel, who shared her experience of publishing. My other American friend, Susanna Gretz, author and illustrator of her delightful children's teddy bear books, was another valued reader of an early draft and has been continuously helpful.

I was also advised in aspects of publishing by retired Commissioning Editor and friend Heather Gibson who with her extraordinary eye for detail carried out a final proof read. Heather also offered advice from her deep reservoir of publishing experience. Another friend from the Tappit Hen days, book Production Manager Roger Hall, also generously provided information and suggestions. Jenny Brown gave of her wealth of publishing knowledge and experience.

Retired nurse and poet, Jan Woods, also read an early draft. Jan straight away honed into asking why nurse Auntie Maisie didn't visit her beloved brother at the Crichton. Of course Maisie did! It took one experienced Scots nurse to read another. Friend Liz Richardson has been consistently supportive, particularly helpful when I was organising the book launch.

The mighty Sheena Wellington, a fellow Dundonian, read the book in one sitting and responded so very encouragingly and warmly. I am honoured that someone with such a deep and thorough knowledge of Scottish history and culture responded so positively.

I owe a life-changing depth of gratitude to the organisers and fellow participants of the ground-breaking Multi-Disciplinary Research Seminars into Psychological Aspects of Eye Disorders at the

Tavistock Clinic, in which I participated for two years. In particular, I acknowledge the organisers and facilitators, the late Dr Alexis Brook (who was a brother of the late, eminent theatre director, Peter Brook) and also Drs Sotiris Zalidis and Andrew Elder. I am profoundly grateful to Sotiris for reading a draft of this book, in spite of being ill, as did former seminar participant and dear friend Eileen Ainsworth. Their responses are deeply valued.

Author and retired teacher of Life Writing classes, Neil Ferguson, suggested attending a life or biography writing class. This led to my attendance at Nicholas Murray's Biography Class at the City Lit. And as can happen in courses much was learnt from the valued participants and this has led to friendships, such as with Helen Pugh.

Zvezdana Popovic, Olga Stanojlovic and Marco Gašić at St Sava's Serbian Orthodox Church, Notting Hill, have been unfailingly generous in their warmth of welcome and in sharing information about Serbia during the First World War, including the terrible typhus pandemic and the awful Great Retreat. I feel honoured to be included in their annual *pomen*, their memorial service to the Scottish Women's Hospitals for Foreign Service who served in Serbia. Zvezdana, probably *the* authority on the Scottish Women's Hospitals, has provided invaluable information about them. These impressive Scottish medical women shared much of the experiences and conditions such as would have been endured by Dr Louis Thomson, and knowledge of them provided me with fascinating background information.

Two loyal local friends have been unstinting in their support and I offer them a special appreciation of gratitude, particularly given their professional experience, warmth and skills. They are Sebastian Balfour, Emeritus Professor of Contemporary Spanish Studies, London School of Economics and Political Science, and Gráinne Palmer, educationalist, and successful businesswoman. Another 'Grove' friend who meticulously advised on local history as well as publishing matters is former Health and Social Services Correspondent of The Times and later its Race Relations and

Disarmament Correspondent, Cllr Pat Healy for Colville ward in London from 1990 to 2002 and St Charles, later Dalgarno, from 2010 to 2022.

I am delighted to have had the help of Mary Turner Thomson of The Book Whisperers. With her exceptional publishing skills of editing, production and design - and much more - Mary has been outstandingly helpful in producing this final product. Mary has also been a pleasure to deal with. Thank you, Mary.

Finally, my companion in this endeavour and in so many others is my husband and resident historian, Terry Statham. Terry's acute intelligence and encyclopaedic knowledge of history has come to my aid so many times. Amongst many journeys, Terry accompanied me on a gruelling trip to the former Western Front area, where two of my uncles had served, and on the less arduous pilgrimage to the French Riviera where my shell shocked uncle 'convalesced'.

By way of a post-script I apologise for any omissions in acknowledgement. That in no way reflects my profound gratitude to all who have helped me. Any failure to show my appreciation is only a reflection of my less than perfect memory.

St Quintin's Kitchen Garden, in the land Princess Louise left to the community

REVIEWS

Eileen Ainsworth, psychotherapist, teacher of visually impaired students, and Mind's Eye researcher: *Beautifully written account...of three brave, magnanimous men. Would make a very moving film.*

Sebastian Balfour, emeritus professor of Contemporary Spanish Studies, London School of Economics and Political Science; researcher on the use of mustard gas by the Spanish in Morocco in the 20s: *...ground-breaking and deeply moving account of aspects of the experience of the First World War and its long-term consequences. It deserves to be widely read ... one of the outstanding qualities of this book: the author's continuous effort to broaden the focus of her biographical account to encompass social history, war studies, memory, and science, particular medical science.*

Dr Tom Harrison, historian of medicine and retired consultant psychiatrist: *A compassionate and reflective account of how soldiering in the First World Wat affected three men and the subsequent mental health of their families ... unusual and perhaps unique account.*

A L Kennedy, writer and academic: *A fascinating meditation on family, war, trauma and Robert Louis Stevenson.*

Sheena Wellington, celebrated singer of traditional Scots song, who memorably sang Robert Burns' 'A man's a man for a' that' at the opening of the Scottish Parliament in 1999: *fascinating story... tragic, intriguing and very moving.*

Jan Woods, retired professional nurse and poet: *well researched ... tells how traditional family ethics of 1914 Scotland affected the lives of her three uncles and herself...duty, faith and silence when faced with pain.*

Dr Sotiris Zalidis, retired GP with an interest in psychosomatic medicine, and author of 'A General Practitioner, his patients and their

feelings: exploring the emotions behind physical symptoms':
...excellent book ...moving and inspiring ... a remarkable achievement ... chapter on the eye and mind... is a good illustration of how far our understanding of psychological trauma has come since the First World War.

AUTHOR PAGE

Born in Broughty Ferry, Liz was first introduced to war trauma at the tender age of twelve when belted by a former prisoner-of-war teacher. Many years later she realised this formed the basis of her awareness of post-traumatic stress disorder. The door was fully opened when she discovered the existence of an unknown Uncle Louis, who had suffered severe and lasting shell shock at the Somme, and was hospitalised for the rest of his life.

Working as an orthoptist Liz developed an interest in inexplicable visual loss. This lead to participation in a multi-disciplinary research project into psychological aspects of eye disorders, followed by a masters in the subject.

During her life's journey she became aware too of the tragedy of Great Uncle James who had been fatally gassed at Ypres; this cast a long shadow over the family.

Liz's final forays into family First World War history revealed the ultimately more uplifting tale of another Louis, cousin Louis Thomson, who had tended to the sufferers of typhus in Serbia in 1915, and had joined the Serbs on their Great Retreat across the mountains of Montenegro and Albania to the Adriatic. He survived to lead a long and fruitful life as a country doctor and social reformer in Burgundy, and left a web of intrigue about his possible royal parentage and his mysterious international activities.